Appalachian Heart

Other Books by Lynn Coffey

Backroads
Plain Folk and Simple Livin'

Backroads 2
The Road to Chicken Holler

Backroads 3
Faces of Appalachia

These books are available through the author's website:
www.backroadsbooks.com

Appalachian Heart

Lynn Coffey

Quarter Books

Cover design by Jane Hagaman
Front cover photograph of
      Napoleon "Po" Fitzgerald Family/Beech Grove, Virginia
Back cover photograph by Lynn Coffey
      of Mary and Frances Cash/Montebello, Virginia
Author photograph by Rebecca Coffey Thompson
All current interior photographs by Lynn Coffey
Family photos in each chapter courtesy of those interviewed
Interior design by Jane Hagaman

Quartet Books
PO Box 4204
Charlottesville, VA 22905
www.quartetbooks.com

If you are unable to order this book from your local bookseller, you may order
directly from the author. Call (540) 949-0329 or use the order form in the
back of the book. For more information about this book or the Backroads
series of books, you may browse Lynn's website at www.backroadsbooks.com.

Library of Congress Control Number: 2013908463

ISBN 978-0-615-77454-1
10 9 8 7 6 5 4 3 2 1
Printed on acid-free paper in Canada

Dedicated to the memory of David Mitchell Coffey, Sr.
A Christian man full of wisdom and godly common sense

David Coffey of Coffeytown, Virginia (September 10, 1936–January 4, 2013)

Contents

Acknowledgments ix

Introduction xi

1. D. Devereaux Davis................................... 1

2. Lila Lee Wilson Campbell 17

3. Lowell Humphreys.................................... 29

4. Mary Bridge Wright and Martha Bridge Ramsey...... 49

5. Ted Hughes 65

6. Agnes Duncan Thompson 81

7. Glenn Allen... 101

8. Madeline White Grant 121

9. Clemon Lee Lawhorne............................. 137

10. Lorean Falls Painter.............................. 157

11. Buck Harris and Lura Coffey Steele 169

12. Frances and Mary Cash 191

13. Icem Lawhorne..................................... 207

14. LaRue Fauber Wilson............................. 225

15. William Henry Coffey............................. 243

16. Ruby Nannie Coffey.............................. 261

Poem: The Chimney Still Stands................... 281

Acknowledgments

As with my other three books about Appalachian culture, there are important people who have helped with the process of completing *Appalachian Heart* and getting it ready for print. Without these special folks, you would not be holding this invaluable book of oral histories—all taken from recordings of Virginia's Blue Ridge Mountain natives.

First and foremost, I'd like to thank God for giving me a talent for writing and the desire for simple living (one that I've possessed since childhood) and for plopping me down smack-dab in the middle of the Blue Ridge Mountains, where I realized I was "home" without ever having lived here before. He gave me a special love for the people of Appalachia, along with the passion and drive needed to capture their unique culture and put it down in print. I am eternally grateful to him for making all my dreams come true.

How could I do the many things connected with writing a book without a loving and supportive husband? I'll tell you . . . I couldn't, and that's why having a man like Billy Coffey by my side has been such a blessing. He's endured more than one late-night supper of scrambled eggs because his wife has been out interviewing a ninety-two-year-old man about bear hunting or a woman in her eighties who's decided to take clogging lessons. God bless you, honey, for your invaluable suggestions, sacrificial love, computer expertise, and, above all, patience!

I thank the girls of Quartet Books for taking me on as the first client in their new publishing services business and making the three Backroads books, as well as this new *Appalachian Heart*, the most attractive self-published books I could ever hope to put my name on. For your valuable input, talent, and willingness to help a virtually unknown author make her work look professional, my gratefulness knows no bounds.

I'd like to also thank Jack Mayer for letting me use a quote from his book, *Life in a Jar: The Irena Sendler Project,* which was one of the most inspirational books I've ever read. Although the quote was about the Jewish people from the Holocaust, the words adequately describe the vanishing mountain culture that, in my own little corner of the world, I am honored to have been a part of preserving.

Last but by no means the least is my undying affection and admiration for the very people that I love to talk to and write about the most: the true natives of the Virginia highlands. It has been my honor and privilege to have lived among them for thirty-three years, and I have more respect for this group of people than anyone I've ever met. Thanks for taking me in and making me a part of your Appalachian hearts—you certainly have captured mine.

Introduction

As I sit here writing the introduction to a book that I'd said I wasn't going to write, I have to smile at that old adage: "Never say never." Actually, I'd said that about the three other books I wasn't going to write, either. You'd think I'd learn. So from now on, I'm simply going to say, "One of these days I'd like to retire," and leave it at that.

Although the content of *Appalachian Heart* is similar to the three Backroads books, there is one difference. *Plain Folk and Simple Livin'*, *The Road to Chicken Holler*, and *Faces of Appalachia* were stories taken from the old *Backroads* newspaper that ran from December 1981 to December 2006. This new book highlights oral histories of the mountain people who are still living and who'd never had their personal life stories included in the other books.

When *Appalachian Heart* switched from a mere idea into an actual reality, I knew exactly who I wanted for my first interview. David Mitchell Coffey, Sr., grew up in the isolated village of Coffeytown, or Alto, as it is also known. David was a very special individual who everyone had the utmost love and respect for, and I couldn't wait to sit down to talk with him about growing up the "old way" in the Virginia mountains. Imagine my sadness when I called his wife, Janie, to set up the interview, and she told me that earlier in the year, David had been diagnosed with a brain tumor and would now be unable to participate. She said that if I had called a few months earlier, he could have talked to me. I was devastated to learn that I had waited too long. This motivated me to move faster in contacting the others I wanted to include in the book.

One positive thing regarding David happened on a cool September morning. Billy and I met David and Janie at their home-place in Coffeytown, just to sit and visit on the porch. I took a few pictures; one of David seemed to capture the essence of the mountain man he was. I later sent the photos to Janie, and she said that she was going to make copies for their children for Christmas. I was honored to see that when David passed away, Janie used that one particular photo at the top of his obituary. In turn, I decided to use that same picture for the dedication page of this book. This experience serves to remind us all not to wait when you feel prompted to talk to someone. Ask questions while you still can . . . while there's still time.

I had several friends tell me that I needed to broaden my horizons when it came to interviewing the mountain people. That I should travel to other parts of the state to capture different dialects and customs from each area. These were good suggestions, but since I'm not much of a traveler, and this is where God plopped me down, and these are the folks I know the best and am most comfortable with, I decided to stick close to home.

It has been such a blessing to talk in depth to these people I've had relationships with all these years but had never known intimate details of their lives. People like Madeline Grant, who became a ward of the state in childhood and lived with many foster families before finding her forever home in Montebello. Or Lila Campbell, whose parents were both deaf mutes and taught their hearing/speaking daughter sign language so that they could communicate. Or Glenn Allen, who fought in the battles of Iwo Jima and Okinawa before returning home to his beloved Blue Ridge Mountains and marrying his sweetheart.

In writing Appalachian Heart, one of the biggest things that stood out while interviewing the mountain people was how considerate they were of the feelings of the people whom they were talking about. I noticed that when I gave them the first draft of their stories to look over for mistakes, most asked to have certain quotes removed or softened lest it cause hard feelings. Even if something they had said wasn't negative, they invariably took the high road when it came to respecting others, rather than try to make themselves look good. Because of this careful proofreading on their part, you can be assured these oral histories are what *they* wanted to say, not what the author wanted them to say, no matter how great the quote.

I've always strived to be honest in my writing and shy away from media sensationalism, which I understand sells. I have been richly rewarded by the mountain people's trust, and that, my friend, is true success. Since moving here, one of the finest compliments I ever received came from Johnny Coffey, my first neighbor here in Love. Johnny said, "Lynn, you write our stories exactly like they were. Why, son, you're just like kinfolk." For me, it doesn't get any better than that.

There were many surprises along the way that made every interview special. I was struck by the originality in how the mountain people named their children. Some were family names that had been handed down through the generations but others were completely novel. The first person I recall with a name that impressed me was Eva Coffey's mother, whom they called "Mint." I thought it was quaint that they'd named her after a wild herb growing in the mountains. Imagine my embarrassment when I found out that her real name was Arminta.

Frances and Mary Cash's great-grandfather was Bingham Mays. The first interview in *Appalachian Heart* is with Devereaux Davis (pronounced DEV-a-row). My all-time favorite name is Icem Lawhorne (pronounced EYE-sum). His name intrigued me so much that I thought if I ever wrote a fictional novel about life in the Blue Ridge, my main character would be a rugged mountain man named Icem. His real-life sister's name, Queenetta, ain't half bad, either!

Each person I interviewed had a few things in common: they were all raised with no modern conveniences, such as electricity or indoor plumbing, and most farmed for a living. But the common threads stop here, as their lives, like the petals of a beautiful flower, unfold before the reader. For those who aren't acquainted firsthand with the mountain culture and have only the media's stereotype of its people being simple, I have this to say. In simplicity is profoundness. And I know that I have been profoundly influenced by each of them.

I believe God gives each person on earth a special gift that he wants us to use to honor him and bless others. He equips us for the job, even if we feel we aren't qualified. All we have to do is be willing. The job he's given me seems to be preserving what's left of the Appalachian culture in my own area. I readily admit that I am not a polished writer and have no aspirations to become a famous author. First and foremost, I remain a mountain housewife with chores that revolve around farm life. I write from the heart about what I know best: the kind and genuine people of the Virginia highlands.

In closing, I'd like to end with a quote from the book *Life in a Jar: The Irena Sendler Project,* by Jack Mayer. My neighbor, Vanessa Fraser, lent me the book, which is based on the true story of a woman from Poland who was responsible for rescuing hundreds of Jewish children during the Holocaust. It is one of the most powerful historical books I've ever read. Although the quote is about the millions of Jewish people exterminated during Hitler's horrific reign, it can also apply to the fast-disappearing Appalachian culture and the reason that this one last book about the mountain people was written.

Everybody has a story. But these people will take their remarkable stories to their graves if we don't uncover them, write them down. That's immortality. We humans—we're storytellers, not that different than when we lived in caves and sat around a fire telling tales. It's the way we make sense of the world. It's what history is.

—Jack Mayer

Appalachian Heart

D. D. Davis

1

D. Devereaux Davis

Billy and I met Devereaux (or "D. D.," as he is known) at Hebron Baptist Church in Afton after Billy became their interim pastor in the summer of 2012. But I had met D. D.'s wife, Alene, back in the early 1980s when she worked at People's Bank of Nelson in Afton. The bank manager at the time was Forest Bryant, Jr., and I got to know all the folks working there when Forest took advertising in the *Backroads* newspaper. I always got a warm welcome when I came through the door, as well as any kind of sweets they had on the break room table. It was one of my favorite spots to stop when delivering the newspapers each month. Who knew that almost thirty years later I would be sitting in Alene's living room interviewing her husband about his early upbringing in the mountains.

That has been the joy of writing the mountain people's histories since December 1981. D. D.'s story was no exception, and although I really didn't know him well when we came to Hebron, one Sunday he mentioned how they got messages to their friends and neighbors up on Stoney Creek long before they had telephones. What he said tickled me so much, I asked if he would consider being a part of *Appalachian Heart* and was delighted when he said yes. I think you readers will be delighted, too.

D. D.'s grandparents on his father's side were Sheffy Lee Davis and Gertrude Thompson Davis. The Thompsons walked out of

Sheffy Lee Davis and his mule, Dan

West Virginia and made their way to Nelson County, Virginia, where they settled up on Stoney Creek. D. D.'s grandfather, Sheffy, married Gertrude, one of the Thompson girls, and Gertrude's brother Powell Thompson married Sheffy's sister, Hattie. With each brother marrying the other's sister, they ended up being double first cousins.

D. D.'s grandparents on his mother's side were George and Rushey English from Zuni, Virginia. During the Depression, D. D.'s father (Delmas Devereaux, Sr.) went to Newport News and got a job working at filling stations during the day; in the evenings he worked for the government collecting gold. He met the

Rushy and George English

Mary George English Davis (D. D.'s mother) as a baby

Englishes's daughter, Mary George English, while employed in Newport News, and she later became his wife.

Delmas later found employment at the DuPont plant in Waynesboro and moved back to Stoney Creek, where he had been raised. D. D. said that all the Davis family members were raised in the same place and only when they became old enough to marry or get jobs, did they, one by one, move off Stoney Creek and into surrounding areas. Before Delmas left for Newport News, he was a cook for the Civilian Conservation Corps while the Blue Ridge Parkway was being constructed just up the mountain behind their homeplace.

Devereaux was born January 28, 1935, the eldest of three children born to Delmas and Mary George Davis. He was born at UVA Hospital in Charlottesville, Virginia, after a harrowing ride on winter roads on which his parents had an accident on the way to the hospital. They slid off old Route 29, hit a tree, and had to

D. D. Davis, Sr., and his siblings

wait until help arrived to cut the tree off the vehicle before they could continue. D. D. has two sisters, Iris and Sandra, who were several years younger than their brother.

D. D. said that when growing up, there was no electricity up on Stoney Creek, but he can remember when they ran the power lines to the old homeplace. In the kitchen, there was a wire that hung down from the ceiling with a light bulb attached to the end of it. "That was amazing, because before that, I sat down many a night to do my homework by lamplight, and when it got dark, we'd just go to bed. Yes, all we had was a bed and a path. . . . You've heard that comment before haven't you?"

When asked what his responsibilities at home were, D. D. laughed and said that his responsibility as the only boy in

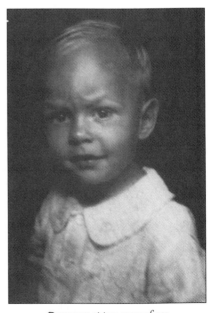

Devereaux at two years of age

the family was to do everything! "I fed and milked the two cows before and after school, fed the hogs and chickens, took care of the horses we used for farm work, plowed the fields, and cut hay with an old sickle mower. My job during hay season was to get in the hay loft and pull in the loose hay Daddy would pitch up with a fork and keep it moving to the back of the barn."

It was at this point in the interview that I asked Devereaux to explain how the people up Stoney Creek got messages back and forth before telephones were installed in their homes. "Where we were living, Wallace Thompson lived across one way, and Thelma McGann and Uncle Powell were up the road the other way. Uncle Jim, the Marshalls, Joe Thomas, and Angus Campbell also lived farther up on Stoney Creek. The Meekses lived in the last house at the top of the mountain before the logging road began. Let's say if we wanted to say something to Angus Campbell, whose wife was part of the Davis family, I'd holler across the field to Thelma, and she'd holler up to Angus. He'd holler back his answer, and that's how we relayed our messages.

"At home, all I had was my two sisters, but Thelma McGann had five boys and a girl, and when I wasn't doing what Daddy made me do, Jimmy, Carl, and Donald, we all played together. We'd fish up Stoney Creek for native trout, plus, when I got a little older, they stocked the creek, too. We would hand fish and also gig them at night, but later on, they outlawed those practices. We'd play cowboys and Indians up in the woods and we'd hunt.

"We had a swimming hole called the buck hole, which was a big pool of water coming down Stoney Creek in front of our home-place. There was a big rock that I'd lay out in the sun on and burn myself up. That's where Wintergreen Christian Church would baptize people. I can remember sometimes after the service they would baptize people and afterward the old folks would sit around eating lunch while us kids would go back and play in the water.

"Back then we didn't have cars, so we walked to church. Cash and Lillie Napier lived way over in the woods from us, and they had five kids. Every Sunday, weather permitting, they would walk to church and come by our house because the road cut right in front of where we lived, and Iris, Sandra, and I would fall in with them. We'd walk down the mountain and pick up Irene Thompson and other people, and, before we got there, we'd have twenty or so people in the group.

"The road up Stoney Creek was about two and a half miles, and it ended at the top where you could drive with a car, but there was an old logging road that continued that one could walk all the way to the Blue Ridge Parkway. When I was a young man, I did some logging up on the mountain. We had horses to pull the logs down to the fields where some landings were built, and the logs were loaded onto old Army vehicles and trucks and taken to Barrett's mill. The Barretts got logging rights to the Big Survey, which was over thirteen thousand acres up where Wintergreen was built."

Here's a little more background history of the land D. D. is describing. In 1952, the land called the "Big Survey" was purchased by North Carolina's William Mattox. Twenty years later, Wintergreen Resort would be developed by Cabot, Cabot & Forbes—the same company involved in the creation of Hilton Head's Sea Pines Resort in South Carolina. D. D. said he can remember that the company sent a man to go all through the mountains, putting out thermometers that were monitored for temperature, and the local people were told there were going to be ski slopes up there. "We laughed at them, talking about building ski slopes up in the mountains. We had a lot of snow back then, but we still couldn't believe it and thought they were crazy."

Christmas was celebrated by cutting down a cedar tree and bringing it back home to be set up and decorated with homemade ornaments. When D. D. was married and had a son of his own, that same tradition was carried on. D. D. and Alene would take young Nathan to Wintergreen, at the bottom of Nellysford, where they had permission to look through the cedars growing there and cut one for their holiday tree. Alene said she always would look for the one that had the best fragrance. They would also look for running cedar and for mistletoe, which grew in the tops of the trees, and shoot a bunch out with a .22 rifle. D. D. recalls that was one of the best Christmas memories he ever had, adding, "Those were the good days."

D. D. said that the family had an old, battery-operated radio; he'd get behind it and pretend he was Santa Claus and talk to his sisters, who would hang on his every word. He remembers the time a man came around wearing a Santa Claus suit. He came in the house and scared D. D. to death. "I ran in the bedroom and crawled up under the bed, and he came and kneeled down by the bed and looked under there at me. He talked a little and rolled me an orange.

"We didn't have much in those days, Lynn. Mama might make a little candy, because there was no such thing as going to the store to buy a pile of candy like they do now. We never saw oranges and bananas until Christmastime and maybe a few nuts. If weather permitted, we'd walk to church for the service. Daddy worked shift work at DuPont and rode a bus, until he got a foreman job and bought a car so he could drive himself back and forth to work."

I asked if his mom cooked a big meal for the holiday. D. D. explained that the family raised their own chickens, and that's what they would have instead of the traditional turkey. "I've butchered many a chicken in my lifetime, and my mama would cook them and put them in half-gallon jars with some syrup, put the top on, and can them. She'd put them in the pantry and all winter long we'd have them along with canned sausage and sauerkraut. . . . You name it and it was in our pantry. We had a big wooden barrel in there filled with flour, and you'd have to dig the weevils out of it so you could cook with it."

The temperatures at that time were much colder, and butchering time always came around Thanksgiving. D. D. said that everyone from the bottom to the head of Stoney Creek had hogs, and everyone would go from place to place to help their neighbors butcher. I asked about lard and was told, "We cooked down the fat to make lard, and I've stood out there many a time and stirred the old pot. We'd get the cracklins and eat those, and they were good. I remember the last butchering I ever did was up at Willard and Thelma McGann's. I went up there to help him and his boys, and after we killed the first hog, it started sleeting. By the time we got the second hog scalded, we like to never got the hair off of it because it was so cold. When the last hog was hung on the pole, there was four inches of snow on the ground.

"Back then it would start snowing around Thanksgiving, and usually you wouldn't see the ground until the end of March. I spent many a day smoking hams, side meat, and shoulders in the smoke-house. We'd have a big tub setting on rocks in the middle of the room, and I'd feed the fire with oak, hickory, or apple wood. You'd have to keep the fires going for two or three days until the meat was completely cured. Mama would send me out with a butcher knife to cut slices off the shoulder meat so she could fry it up for breakfast. We'd grind up all the sausage and Mama would can it."

D. D. attended the old Rockfish School, which had eleven grades. He drove the bus during his last couple of years of high school. "There was no such thing as a drop of snow hitting the ground, and they'd cancel school. No, ma'am; I'd have to get out there and put the chains on."

In the middle of his senior year, D. D. enlisted in the Naval Reserve. He was only seventeen, and his daddy said that the only way he would sign for him to go into the Navy was if he would finish school, so the Navy gave him a six-month defer-ment. "I graduated in 1953, and at that time was the only male member of my family to ever graduate. The Korean War was still going, but by the time I finished school, the war had ended and every-one was coming back. I had enlisted for eight years; two years active and six years inactive, but when Eisenhower became president, he said that everyone who had enlisted for eight years prior to 1955 would not be obligated to pull that two years active duty.

"I stayed in the Naval Reserve for twelve years, and by that time, I was mar-

Devereaux as an eighteen-year-old Naval Reservist

ried and our son was coming along, so I never reenlisted after that. After graduation, I got a job at Wilson Trucking as a truck driver and worked for them for four years. It was right about this time DuPont started hiring, and I went to my boss, Mr. C. W. Wilson, and told him I'd like to try and get a job over there. I went and had my interview and my physical and got hired and went and told him. He said to me, 'Go up to Mrs. Bridgewater and tell her to give you your check and give you a week's vacation,' and he wished me well."

D. D. said at first he caught rides to work with different people who had cars, but later he bought one of his own: a 1931 Model A Ford that he sold when he and Alene "went to housekeeping"; that is, set up house on their own.

Alene's father, Willie Wesley Farrar (1893–1973)   Alene's mother, Grace Wood Farrar (1901–1997)

It was at this point that Alene gave me a bit of her family history as well. She came into the world on December 9, 1936, the last child of six to be born to Willie "Bill" W. Farrar and Grace Esther Wood Farrar. At one time, Willie ran a stave mill in the Adial area that made wooden barrels. Alene's siblings, in the order of their birth, were Virginia, Willie, Wesley, Annie, and John. Alene is the last surviving of the six children.

Alene's grandparents on her father's side were John William Farrar and Minnie Belle Critzer Farrar, who lived and farmed in the Avon area.

On her mother's side, her grandparents were Tillie Wood and Sallie Powell Wood, who started out living in Adial and later moved to Lynchburg where they ran a boarding house.

Alene attended Rockfish School, but her older broth-

Alene with her brother John

ers and sisters went to the wooden schoolhouse located behind Rodes United Methodist Church in Avon, which was closed by the time Alene started school.

I asked D. D. how he had met his wife. He smiled and said, "She was a blind date." Alene, in the background, smiled back and added, "I was everybody's blind date . . . the 'fill in' when a boy or girl wanted to go out with a special person, and they needed

John William Farrar and Minnie Belle Critzer Farrar

another couple to go along."

Farrar family members

I asked what a typical date would be, and they said that they would go to the Dairy Bar in Waynesboro to get hamburgers and a milk shake before going to the Skyline Drive-In Theater, out on Route 250. Sometimes they would go to the indoor theaters, the Wayne or the Cavalier, but mostly they went to the drive-ins because they showed the best movies.

Going back a little further, D. D. said that Mr. Landon Phillips ran a drive-in movie theater in Beech Grove at the corner of Routes 664 and 151. Mr. Phillips also ran a little store across the

Tillie Wood and Sallie Powell Wood

The Wood family members (Alene is the small child at the left)

road from the theater. D. D. remembers that a man by the name of Crawford had a big flatbed truck. He'd drive up Stoney Creek; all the kids would pile on the back, and he'd carry them to the movies. D. D. remembers that the drive-in charged twenty-five cents to get in, then they'd sit on the ground to watch the film.

"We didn't have a lot of entertainment back then, and all those people on Stoney Creek on Saturday nights, they used to get together and have a dance. My daddy's house was one of the biggest houses up there, and they would carry all the furniture out of the house and put it outdoors and then get in there and have a dance. I've sat in the corner many a night and just watched the people and listened to the music. They'd have guitars and banjos and stuff like that and have a knock-down, drag-out dance. Of course they'd have a little moonshine that come off of Piney River."

D. D. and Alene courted for a little over a year. They were married on February 6, 1954, at the Wintergreen Christian Church by Rev. Elwood Campbell, who was related to them and was the pastor at both the Beech Grove and Wintergreen Christian Churches at the time. Alene wore a navy blue suit, navy shoes, and a fancy little white hat trimmed in navy. Alene said that her mama used to say, "If you wear blue, he'll stay true."

D. D.'s daddy took him to town and bought him a blue suit and gave him twenty dollars for his wedding. After they were married, they picked up another couple and drove to Waynesboro to celebrate by going to the Dairy Bar to get something to eat and—you guessed it—the Skyline Drive-In Theater to take in a movie.

After marriage, the Davises lived with Alene's mother for about a year. During that time, their only child, Nathan, was born. He was born at the old Waynesboro Hospital, which was then located in the present-day McDow Funeral Home building. Alene remembers that she stayed in the hospital for five full days before returning home with her newborn son. After Nathan was born, D. D. sold the Model A car, and, with the money, the couple struck out on their own to set up housekeeping in a two-room apartment above a store run by the Small family in Nellysford.

From there, they moved to Beech Grove and rented a brick home owned by Paige Grove. When D. D. began working at DuPont, they moved to a little house up the mountain on Route 6, sandwiched between Alene's mother and sister. They moved to their present home in Afton in 1963. D. D.'s father signed a note for a construction loan at the First National Bank, and they hired Coy Anderson to frame the house and put in the windows.

After that, they built piecemeal, hiring different people to do various jobs. Alene's father, Willie, was a master carpenter and taught D. D. how to build cabinets and trim work. Alene's brother Wesley did the exterior brickwork, and her brother John finished the interior sheetrock. D. D. gained more construction experience by working with Clifton Anderson, who was a cabinet maker by profession. The Davis's home is filled with beautiful cabinetry that D. D. added through the years.

I've learned that by talking more in depth with people, you find out all sorts of surprising facts that would go unnoticed in everyday conversation. For instance, we had a Christmas program at Hebron in 2012, and the question was asked, "What was your favorite Christmas memory." I spoke up and said it was when I asked for a Red Ryder B. B. gun and a bow and arrow set when I was twelve.

This spurred D. D. to tell me that he and Alene had belonged to an archery club when they were younger, and together they'd competed in bow shoots around the state, garnering many trophies and patches for their competitive shooting. While I was at their house, D. D. went to the basement and brought up the recurve bows they'd used while participating in archery tournaments. D. D.'s foreman at DuPont was a lady by the name of Fanny Lilly, and she and her husband, Larry, had introduced them to the sport. Larry had made D. D. a bow from bird's-eye maple and mahogany wood, and it is a beautiful piece of workmanship.

The Davises have been members of Hebron Baptist Church for most of their married life, although they've always had family ties

Davis family portrait

to both Wintergreen Christian and Adial Baptist churches. They are active Christians, and D. D. is on the board of deacons at Hebron, along with his son, Nathan.

Nathan is very talented in many areas. He is a consummate artist in painting and pencil drawing, has decorating skills, has a beautiful singing voice, and his parents told me that he is an excellent cook, as well. Billy and I were awestruck the week after Thanksgiving when we came into

Hebron Church and saw all the beautiful Christmas decorations Nathan had placed in the vestibule and sanctuary. He clearly has been blessed with special gifts that he willingly gives from his heart to others. Nathan is employed in the library at Rockfish Elementary School and has been married going on twenty-six years to Teresa Anderson Davis, who is employed at Augusta Health. They have one daughter, Natalie Rose, who is now eleven.

Devereaux and Alene at home

D. D. retired as a maintenance supervisor from DuPont in 1991, after thirty-four and a half years of service. Alene retired with twenty-three years of service from the bank that began as People's Bank of Nelson, was later changed to F&M, and is now BB&T. She loves to crochet and now makes keepsake baby caps for the Augusta Health nursery in Fishersville.

Winding down the afternoon, I asked one last question about growing up on Stoney Creek, and D. D. volunteered, "We didn't buy fancy automobiles or other big things. We just lived a normal life and that's . . . that."

Lila Lee Campbell at her Tyro home

2

Lila Lee Wilson Campbell

I t was a perfect autumn afternoon when I drove to Lila's house to talk with her. The temperature was cool, the sky was October blue, and the fall leaves were at their peak of color. I have to travel down Campbell's Mountain Road—one of the last gravel mountain roads left in our area—to get to Lila's. I know people who positively will not drive down the steep narrow road, but we take it in stride because we travel it so frequently.

The wind was really whipping the day of the interview, and I drove through a never-ending swirl of falling leaves that left me breathless with its beauty. Lila's big grey-and-white kitty met me outside and promptly flopped over on his side for a good scratch behind the ears. Lila answered the back door. It's funny how everyone here always goes to the back door. Anyone coming to the front door is either "company" or a salesman. Country folk visit via the back door and always get a welcoming greeting. Today was no different.

I've known Lila so long, I can't recall when we first met. Probably after I started writing the *Backroads* newspaper and began going to all the activities held in the mountains. She was always at the Montebello and Fleetwood horse rides, usually held at a rescue squad or school, cooking something delicious in their kitchens. She came to family reunions and church functions. I knew her face before knowing her name. But I really got to know

Lila; her husband, Harold; and their three children when Billy and I began attending Cornerstone Baptist Church in Tyro in the 1990s. Lila was, and continues to be, an active member of the church, lending a helping hand with anything that's needed. I knew that she had a particularly interesting story, and it was a joy to sit with her and hear all the details of it. So fix yourself a cup of coffee, get comfy, and enjoy Lila Campbell's amazing life.

Lila Lee Wilson was born on January 18, 1930, the only child of Clarence Everett Wilson and Mattie Alice Snead Wilson.

Clarence and Mattie Wilson, Lila's parents

Lila's father was from West Virginia and worked in the coal mines as a young man before moving to Virginia. Her mother was born in Augusta County, Virginia, and most of her people were from that area.

Clarence and Mattie had met at a reunion held at the Virginia School for the Deaf and Blind (VSDB) in Staunton, Virginia, where Mattie had been a student. You see, both of Lila's parents were deaf mutes. Her father had been handicapped since birth, and her mother, who had started out speaking and hearing normally, climbed on a chair as a toddler and drank some lye that her mother had kept on a shelf. The lye ate through Mattie's vocal chords and affected her hearing. It was a miracle she even lived. When she was older, she got a job at the Craddock/Terry Shoe Factory in Lynchburg and worked there for a long time.

After the school reunion, the couple began seeing each other and fell in love. They married when Mattie was in her thirties. Clarence was ten years older than his bride. The Wilsons moved to

William Henry Wilson,
Lila's paternal grandfather

James Sterling Clayborne Snead,
Lila's maternal grandfather

Richmond, where Clarence found employment at the Lane Cedar Factory. Lila was born in Richmond at Sheltering Arms Hospital. She said that her mother had a hard time delivering her and ended up having a cesarean section, which was quite a difficult operation at that time.

These were the years of the Great Depression, and the cedar factory eventually closed down. When Lila was three years of age, the family decided to come to Tyro. They moved in with Mattie's half-sister, Lillie; her husband, Bruce Nash; and Bruce's brother Mixen. The Nash home was large enough to accommodate the six people living there. It had an upstairs with four bedrooms, so everyone had their own

Lila on her mother's lap

room. However, electricity and indoor plumbing were still years away, and the families lived in the way their ancestors had.

As a child, Lila's parents taught her sign language, and this was the principal way in which they communicated. When the Wilsons first came to Tyro, the Nashes thought that Lila was also a deaf mute because she never spoke. Once she was around speaking people, however, Lila quickly adapted and learned spoken language. She was then able to converse in two ways: by signing with her parents and by talking with her aunt and uncles. Early photos of Lila at a young age show that she wore her hair in long sausage curls, a style she continued to wear for many years.

Lila as a child   Lila with Leonard Snead

Although Lila, at four years of age, was too young to attend school, a teacher by the name of Miss Sanford would stop by her home and take her to the two-room schoolhouse located next to Harmony Church so that she could sit in with the bigger girls. When she was actually old enough to go to classes, she attended Fleetwood in Massies Mill that taught grades one to eleven.

The Nash family owned and operated a large apple orchard and packing shed. Lila said that she remembers how they would hook horse teams up to ground sleds loaded with wooden barrels and drive them to the orchard where the pickers would pack fruit in them during the fall harvest. One day, when no one was looking, Lila climbed into one of the empty barrels, and it began to roll down the hill. People started yelling and chasing after it,

fearful that if it made it to the Tye River, Lila would be washed downriver. Luckily, they caught it before she got to the water, and that was the last time she climbed into an apple barrel! She said that each weekend during apple-picking time, the family would drive to Lynchburg to sell fruit, butter, and eggs at the farmer's market.

Lila as a young girl

Lila met her husband, Harold Campbell, when he came to the orchard seeking employment. The Campbells lived about halfway down Campbell's Mountain in a home that Harold's father had built. The house still stands and is occupied today. Harold's parents were Clarence Campbell and Bucy Hatter Campbell.

Harold in his naval uniform

After his stint at the orchard, Harold found a job at Craddock/Terry Shoe Factory in Lynchburg, the same company that Lila's mother had worked for years before.

In 1945, Harold joined the Navy; when he came home from boot camp, he and Lila married. They tied the knot on March 8, 1945, and were married by Rev. Longwood at the Methodist parsonage in Lovingston, Virginia. Lila remembers that she wore a blue dress with white trim and white shoes. Harold was dashing in his Navy uniform. They came back to live in the Nash house before Harold left for Bainbridge Naval Station in Miami, Florida, where he was stationed.

Lila, as a young bride, boarded the train accompanied by her aunt Lillie and made the long trip down to Florida to be with her new husband. What a big adventure for a young lady. She remembers eating in the train dining car and looking out the windows, marveling at the brand-new chapter of life she was about to enter. In Georgia, she said that little children would line the track and wait for people to toss pennies out to them. Once in Miami, Lila said it was such a busy, different world from the quiet one she left back in Tyro. (Fast forward to just a few short years ago when Lila said that she and her daughter, Linda, made the same trip down to Miami, only to be

Newlyweds Harold and Lila

completely disoriented because of the changes that had occurred in the sixty-seven years since she had lived there.)

The couple lived off base and didn't have a lot of money, so Harold brought his bride something to eat from the commissary when he came home for the evening. When Harold was transferred to another base, Lila came back home to Tyro. A year later, the war ended, and Harold came home for good.

He worked on the Nash farm, then later found a job as a taxi driver in Lynchburg, where they moved. Their first child, Linda, was born on August 5, 1947. Shortly thereafter, the Campbells

Bruce Nash, Mixen Nash, and Harold Campbell

bought the old John Hatter homeplace on Route 56, just up the road from the Nash house. Their first son, Tom, was born on June 16, 1950, in the home that Lila still occupies. She remembers that Leasy Snead Adams, her mother's sister, was the midwife living on Harper's Creek; she delivered Tom as well as most of the children in the Tyro area.

Linda attended Fleetwood School and finished high school at S.V.A. in New Market, going on to college in Maryland. Tom also attended Fleetwood and right out of high school, he went to work for Jennings, a company in northern Virginia that did construction and landscaping. Later he worked for his brother-in-law, Carl Coffey, who also had a successful business in that area. When Tom retired, he moved back to Tyro to a home right down the road from his mother. Lila said his home used to be a schoolhouse from an earlier time.

Lila's last child, Mark, was born in the Waynesboro hospital on May 12, 1966. He attended the school at Massies Mill for part of the elementary grades, then fourth through seventh grades at

C. F. Richards in Staunton, and graduated from Nelson County High School. He later went to college and graduated from Virginia Tech in Blacksburg.

Three years after Mark's birth, on the night of August 19, 1969, Hurricane Camille ripped through Nelson County, taking many lives and causing untold devastation to the area. Lila said that it was raining so hard that sometime after midnight she asked Harold to get up and look outside. He went to the door and the rising water was already up to his knees. He told Lila to bundle up Mark and put him in the family Volkswagen; they drove up the back side of the mountain and parked.

Lila recalled, "The lightning was continuous, and the thunder so loud you had to holler loud just to be heard inside the car. When daylight came, we could see where the river had come across the road and into the basement of our house. A huge landslide came right beside us in the car, and we never knew it until the following morning.

"Our house was located in a bad place: between Coxes Creek and the Tye River. The abutment from the old Hatter gristmill, which was located on our property and powered by Coxes Creek, got washed away. We could see washing machines and all kinds of other debris floating down the river. What saved our house was debris that had wedged in the rocks along the creek, diverting the water away from where we lived. It washed out two big culvert pipes on Route 56 and much of the road on Coxes Creek, trapping those who lived up the hollow.

"After talking with Aunt Lillie, the phone went dead, so Harold decided to walk down to see if she and my mother were [still] okay. Trees were down everywhere, and he walked across one that had fallen over the creek and hopped to the other side, making his way down to the Nash place where they lived. There was four foot of mud inside the downstairs of the house, and all the windows were washed out. My aunt woke up in the middle of the night, and knew they could never make it out, so they went upstairs to wait out the storm. That's where Harold found them, shaken up but still alive.

"A home across the road that belonged to the Zirkles had washed completely across Route 56 and came to rest in Aunt Lillie's field. The Mennonites came after the storm and shoveled out all the mud and pulled out the furniture that was still good and put in new windows. They did so much for so many after the storm, and I can't say enough about how grateful we all were."

By this time Harold was cutting timber and milling it at his sawmill, but the mill was also taken by the storm. So he bought a dump truck and began helping with the reconstruction work of Route 56. This turned into a hauling business that he eventually retired from. He also drove the handicapped bus for Nelson County Schools.

When Tom was in the third grade, Lila began working for the Nelson County School system as the school's janitor, driving a school bus, and working in the cafeteria. She started in September 1959 and retired in June 1995, after some thirty years of service. She also worked summers at the Seventh Day Adventist Camp in Montebello when school was not in session.

When the children were growing up, the family attended Evergreen Christian Church at Nash, not far from their home. Later they went to the Adventist Church in Staunton, and finally settled at Cornerstone Baptist Church in Tyro, where Rev. Jerry Hopkins was pastor.

The Snead family reunion in 1951

Lila said that her dad could draw most anything, and when she was small, he let her doodle on paper, encouraging her artwork. In the late 1980s, Lila began attending art classes taught by Eleanor Fauber in an old schoolhouse near Brownsburg, Virginia. Later, those same people began to meet in the basement of Mount Paran Baptist Church in Montebello. Eleanor moved to Pennsylvania after her husband Ray passed away, but the class members continue to meet each Wednesday morning at Mount Paran. When one walks through Lila's home, there is ample evidence of her artwork: beautiful oil paintings depicting landmarks in the Tyro area around her home, the one-room Tyro School, the Nash home, Harold's old truck overgrown with honeysuckle, and many still lifes. When my husband, Billy, was the pastor at Cornerstone Baptist Church, Lila presented us with an oil painting of the church that we still treasure.

Lila's parents lived in the Nash house for the rest of their lives. Bruce Nash died first, followed by his brother Mixen, then Clarence, Lila's aunt Lillie, and finally Mattie. But Lila's mother and her aunt lived there together for many years after the men had passed away.

Harold passed away in March 1997, after fifty-three years of marriage. Lila misses him still. At the last count, in addition to her children, Lila now has five grandchildren and three great-grandchildren. Framed pictures of her lovely family hang on the walls and stand on tables of her home, and it is clear that she loves each one dearly.

As we rooted through boxes of early photos, picking special ones for this chapter, I asked Lila what she thought the biggest change has been during her eighty-two years of living. Without hesitation she replied, "Discipline! Everything is moving too fast with technology and parents working. They are so busy, they don't take the time to discipline their children anymore. Also, people don't visit and associate with each other anymore.

"I remember Aunt Lillie had a quilting room upstairs, and people would come and spend all day talking and quilting together. Neighbors would come and sit on the porch and talk. It's nothing like it used to be. It wasn't all this fast living and rushing around. Tom and the other children would go out and play up and down the creek bank, and we never thought nothing of it. Now I'd be afraid to let them out of my sight."

As we ended the interview, I asked Lila if I could take her picture, and she asked where I wanted her to stand. In the kitchen . . . by the massive Home Comfort wood-burning cookstove with fresh biscuits sitting on top. A sweet smile; a snapped photo; a moment in time capturing not only the essence of a special woman but of an era where fresh biscuits atop a wood stove were the norm.

Lowell Humphreys

3

Lowell Humphreys

I met Lowell and his wife, Viola, back in 1986 when Lowell killed one of the first coyotes in our area. The big male weighed more than fifty pounds and had killed forty-eight of Aubrey Bradley's spring lambs before it was shot. Then in April 1989, I did a story about Skylark Farm, where the Humphreys lived, and we that's where our friendship began. A few years later, Lowell once again made the pages of *Backroads* when he captured a

Mousy and her babies

wild hog and tamed her. "Mousy" had a litter of piglets, one of which was a male that Lowell named "Shotgun Red," and I snapped many a photo of him and Red together.

Shotgun Red

When Billy and I married, the friendship with the Humphreys blossomed further because Lowell had worked with Billy's dad on the Parkway, and they knew each other from years back. I guess the relationship was firmly cemented when Billy began pastoring at Mount Paran Baptist Church in Montebello, where Lowell and Viola attended. Both men have birthdays at the end of May, and many times we'd celebrate and go out to eat together.

Lowell with Shotgun Red

I featured Viola in my first book, *Back-roads: Plain Folk and Simple Livin'*, when she showed folks how to churn butter. It is now my pleasure to write about Lowell and his early life plus the special talent he inherited from his father. Lowell Humphreys, like his daddy, Frank, is a consummate storyteller; a man with the ability to make you laugh so hard, you find yourself begging him to stop for a minute just so you can catch your breath and wipe the tears from your eyes. We all love him, and I know you will, too!

Lowell came into the world on May 30, 1942, the eighth of ten children born to Frank Swanson Humphreys and his wife, Deanie Lou Maddox Humphreys, the daughter of Marion and Rosa Lee Maddox. Frank's father, Marion Lewis "Tip" Humphreys, was from Coffeytown. He was a master carpenter who'd helped build the Macedonia Church there. The interior of the one-room chapel has always struck me as one of the most beautiful works of bead-board placement that I've ever seen. The back of the church where the pulpit stands is a work of art, as are the walls that have various patterns throughout the interior.

Lowell said that his grandfather had done all the fancy work with hand tools of the era and trained many area men in fine carpentry, who then went on to become highly sought after in the building trade. Tip died in 1908 when his son Frank was only four years old. Lowell's grandparents on his mother's side lived in Amherst County at the head of Little Piney.

Lowell's paternal grandfather, "Tip" Humphreys, on the left back row holding one of his children

Frank and Deanie met at a dance, began their courtship and married in September 1926. At the time, Frank was staying with Henry Coffey, who lived at what was called the "Hog Camp" at the head of Big Piney River near Coffeytown. The newlyweds continued to live with Henry for a time.

Frank was a logger and a farmer and was what was known as a "teamster," a man who drives a team of horses. Lowell said, "If people had a balky horse, they'd call my daddy to come straighten it out. Daddy told the story about Mr. Willie Seaman having two gray mares by the names of Bessie and Mary. Bess would always balk on a hard pull. Willie's son, Julian, told Daddy, 'When old Bess comes out of that sag on the lower railroad, she's gonna balk.' Frank said, 'Let me get up on her side, and you hand me a pole, and I'll make her go on out of there.'

"When she started rearing up, my daddy, who was a big strong man, hit her in the side with the pole a couple of licks. He cut the blinder off her bridle on the side where she could see him and the next time they come down, Daddy had hold of the lines [reins] and was resting her there for a minute, but ol' Bess started pulling that log before Mary ever got started!

"When Willie Seaman came down to see how they were getting along, Daddy told him about what he had done. Willie said, 'If I would have known all you had to do was cut the blind off Bessie's bridle, I would have done that years ago.' Julian told his father, 'Pa, that ain't what done it!'

"At the time, Route 56 was just a narrow wagon road, and Willie contracted to widen it from the top of the Parkway to the forks of the Tye River. Daddy was hired to drive Willie's team of horses because he was the only one who could work ol' Bess. There was no big mechanical equipment to work with back then, and they shoveled the dirt from the road with a horse-drawn wooden scoop. It took them several years to finish that few miles of distance."

The Humphreyses lived at the Henry Coffey place for about a year before moving to a little place they called Sweet Briar. It had been part of a girls' camp that the Sweet Briar College had owned, and that's where their first child, Eunice, was born in 1927.

During this time, there were dinky railroads winding through the mountains that were owned by large lumber companies. The people who were employed by these companies to cut logs from large tracts of land were given wooden shanties to live in. Frank got a job logging, and he and Deanie followed the log train to each new location. When one tract was logged out, the shanties would be loaded onto the train and moved to the next location. The cut timber was brought down the mountain, loaded on the train, then hauled to the South River Lumber Company in Cornwall, Virginia, where it was milled. Lowell's oldest brother "Buck" was born in Cales' Hollow, where they were logging at the time.

Soon after Buck's birth, Mr. Norm Ropp, who was the head man at the lumber company, decided he wanted to go into the cattle business, so he and Frank quit logging to raise Shorthorn cattle. Lowell's sister Georgia was born in Coffeytown at Mr. Ropp's place. Lowell said that later, "Daddy bought the old Mike Cash place, and that's where my parents were living when my sister Elizabeth and my two brothers Frank, Jr. (whom they called Bill) and Jesse were born. Horses were scarce to find back then and expensive, so there wasn't too many to be had. So my daddy broke some oxen to work from the herd of Shorthorn cattle he raised. Buck and Bill were the names of the oxen. You have to give oxen plenty of time to work. They are not as fast as horses, and if you push them, they'll get too hot on you."

Frank and Deanie then bought the old Ramsey homeplace, which was just a short way down the mountain from where the Cash property was located. Lowell and his younger siblings were born there. The ten Humphrey children, in the order of their births, are as follows: Eunice in 1927, Norman ("Buck") in 1929, Elizabeth ("Pete") in 1931, Georgia in 1934, Frank (Bill) in 1936, Jesse in 1938, Marion in 1940, Lowell in 1942, Robert in 1947, and Shirlyn in 1953.

In 1954, the family made one more move to some land bought from George Campbell. They built the home in which they continued to live until Frank died. Lowell's daddy passed

Five of the Humphreys children:
Elizabeth, Jesse, Marion, Bill, and Lowell

away January 16, 1986; Deanie stayed on in the home until around 1995 when she came out to live with Lowell and Viola, who were living at Skylark Farm at the time.

Lowell and Viola now own the Humphreyses' last family homeplace, and they built a new home on the property where they moved after retirement. Out by the gravel road running by their place stands a sign that once graced the entrance of their Sky-lark home, announcing where Lowell Humphreys, farm manager, lived. "Since no one else by that name was going to live at Skylark anymore, I just took the sign with me when I left," Lowell said.

Going back to the early years of Lowell's life, I asked where he went to school while growing up. He said that he attended the two-room schoolhouse in Montebello that covered grades one through eight. I was surprised to learn that he did not walk to school but rode a bus driven by Mr. Tom Byers that came up Painter's Mountain Road where he lived. Lowell said that besides his brothers and sisters, the Wheeler children also rode the bus, as did Clarence Campbell's family. The Campbells lived way up across the Park-way, and their children would have to walk down to where the bus picked them up, sometimes in snow up to their knees. "We had bad winters then," recalled Lowell.

"Marie Seaman was my first teacher, and Miss Hawkins, who was an old-maid school teacher, had a lot of fun in her. I also had a teacher by the name of Mrs. Johnson at the Montebello School.

Most of the teachers boarded with either the Tom Byers family or Jake Anderson. I went to the Montebello School through the sixth grade, and when it closed, we had to go to the Fleetwood School in Massies Mill. I went to Fleetwood for the seventh grade and finished up at Nelson County High School, attending the eighth through the tenth grades before starting my first paying job."

Lowell and his farm manager sign

As a child, some of Lowell's chores at home were chopping wood, milking the cows, feeding the hogs and chickens, and gathering the eggs. He said that they always had two or three cows, one of which was called a stripper. A stripper, he explained, was a cow that didn't give much milk but wasn't bred back, so they could milk her all winter and have a little coming in until the other cows came fresh. He said that most everyone had cows because you couldn't buy milk at the stores.

He remembers that Albert Farris, Parrish Robertson, and Flora Grant all ran general mercantile stores in the area when he was a young boy. "Back then, you didn't need much; a little coffee, sugar, salt, and maybe

Lowell at eleven years old

some baking powder. When we moved out to the house where I was born, we didn't have many outbuildings, but when they lived back at the red house [the Ramsey homeplace], there was a spring house and a ground house with a smoke house on top of it. They kept fruit and some potatoes in the ground house, and sometimes they'd bury the potatoes in the ground itself.

"I've heard my daddy tell about his grandmother making apple butter and putting it loose in a special place made for it, and a thick skim would come over the top maybe three-quarters of an inch thick. If you wanted some, you'd cut a square out and dip some of the apple butter out under the plug, and then it would seal back over. And Mama would make what they called 'leather britches,' which was pole beans strung together and dried. You had to soak them right smart before cooking them. I never did like them much—they're kind of tough—but Daddy liked them on a snowy day. He'd tell Mama, 'Why we ought to try some of those leather britches today.'"

Lowell said that his brother Marion went to work at sixteen years of age building the Parkway from Route 60 down by the tunnel. Men weren't supposed to work there until they were eighteen years old, but they thought he was of age so they hired him. Lowell said, "That didn't leave anyone to help with the farm work but me and Elizabeth. We cut the hay up near the Parkway, and all we had back then was a hay loader and no baler. We'd put up that hay loose, and it was slippery, and you'd have to pack it just right or it would slide off the wagon.

"Daddy would be up driving that tractor and would try to get as much of it done as he could, and he'd like to have worked us kids to death! We'd bring it in to the barn, where we had a hay fork to pull it up to the haymow. I'd have to go way in the back of the loft to pull the loose hay back before bringing another load up. It sure was hard work."

Lowell got his first paying job at sixteen, working with Billy Byers at his sawmill and skidding logs for five dollars a day. When Lowell first started, he was the off-bearer, someone who took the cut slabs off the saw platform and piled lumber in stacks. Lowell then began helping Billy roll the big logs over on the carriage so he could slab them off.

"We'd cut logs off Rich Holler, which was real steep. Billy had an old 1953 Chevy truck, and we'd put too much on it sometimes, and we'd get nearly to the top of the hill and the truck would choke out. Well, suh, when Billy would hit the brakes, she'd fly around with you! Billy's daddy, Tom, didn't want to unload all the logs and would say, 'Let's get a pole, and me and Lowell will get on the end of the pole and hook it under the bumper.' We'd get way out on the end and ride that thing up the mountain. I didn't weigh much, but Tom was a big stout man, and when the truck would choke out, I'd jump off, but Tom would ride it out, and it would carry him way up in the air and throw him off down the hill. In the fall, we'd quit work a little early, and we'd go down Edsel Hollow and kill us a mess of squirrels.

"When I was seventeen years old, three of my brothers were working at the paper mill in Buena Vista. A job opening came up, and I went to work there. They put you on one of the messiest jobs there was to start with to see if you were going to stay. I started out as a pot washer, cleaning the large vats of "dope," which is a chemical they mixed with color to dye suitcases. From there I went on to the printers with my brother Marion. The machine would put a design like cowhide or a dapple on the paper as it was run through and then used for imitation leather on luggage. I worked there until I was around twenty and then quit to help Daddy back on the farm.

"I also helped Edgar Austin, the boss-man on the Parkway, cut out the overlooks with a chain saw from April to July that year. I picked a few apples that fall, and when I turned twenty-one, I went back to the paper mill and worked there until the spring of 1967. I quit the paper mill and got a seasonal job on the Parkway until the season closed that fall, and in November, Ral Satterwhite got me a job spraying the electric lines for the Central Virginia line. I worked at that until February 1968. In March, I went back to the Parkway and they had me cutting brush."

I asked Lowell when he and Viola had married. Without hesitation, he answered, "August 15, 1964." One thing I was impressed with was how Lowell knew exact dates of all the milestones in his life. We are all getting to the age when we have to think on these things for a bit before we can remember, but Lowell knew all the important dates immediately.

He and Viola more or less grew up together and were childhood sweethearts all along. When I asked when he started dating his future wife, Lowell laughed and said, "Ever since I was eleven years old!" Viola's parents were John and Ivetta Mays, who lived back on Jack's Hill near the Dickie Brothers' Orchard in Massies Mill. Viola's sister, Velma, married Lowell's brother Buck, so as it ended up, two brothers married two sisters. In February 1964, Viola went to stay with her sister in Richmond, working a factory job that she said she hated. It wasn't long before she called her family and asked them to come get her. Lowell surprised Viola by riding along with them, and soon after they began seeing more of each other on a regular basis. They were married that same summer.

The couple moved to Buena Vista, where Lowell was still working at the paper mill, but in December 1964, they moved back to the mountains and set up housekeeping in the old Ramsey home (called the "red" house because of the color it was painted). Their only child, Lowell Edward Humphreys, Jr., was born in the Lexington Hospital. L. E. arrived on November 15, 1965, the same day his mother had twenty years earlier. Lowell said of the move back to the mountains, "I had enough of city life. I like to get out and hunt when I want to, and I like to get out and just holler."

The family lived at the Ramsey homeplace until June 1970. That's when Harry Fauber, a man the Humphreyses had known for a long time, came to ask Lowell if he'd be interested in becoming the farm manager at Harry's former home. Harry had bought his family homeplace and acreage that bordered Spy Run Gap and the Blue Ridge Parkway but later sold it to a man by the name of Timmons. In 1962, Lowell and his father plowed up the back part of the property for the Christmas trees Timmons wanted to plant and sell. The 365 acres was later sold to Mr. Leslie Cheek, an heir to the Maxwell House coffee company, who lived in Richmond. When Cheek asked Harry, the former owner of the land, if he knew of anyone who he might hire to be the caretaker at the farm, Harry immediately thought of Lowell.

The Humphreyses made the move to Skylark Farm and resided there for almost forty years. At first they lived in the basement of a home the Cheeks had built as a summer retreat. Another home was built in 1977 as a private residence for Lowell, Viola, and their son. Growing up, L. E. had the good fortune to be a young man

Lowell, Viola, and L. E. (August 1967)

surrounded by a 365-acre kingdom. He later married Kim Law, and their cozy mountain home is just across the road from where L. E.'s parents now live.

Lowell said that Mr. Cheek always had a list of things that needed to be done around the farm. From doing odd jobs around the various buildings and constructing fences to cutting grass and trimming the Christmas trees, there was always a project needing to be done. In the early days, Viola did a lot of the cooking and cleaning for the Cheeks when they would come up for a stay.

In July 1977, the mountaintop farm was given to the college of Washington and Lee; Lowell and Viola stayed on as caretakers until their retirement. The land was recently sold once again to a private individual, who continues to enjoy the vast beauty of the property.

Like his father before him, Lowell has always had a love of good horseflesh. He has ridden most of his life and continues to keep a massive Percheron/Shire cross workhorse named "Pocahontas." She was loose in the pasture the day I took their picture together, and when Lowell called her, the horse ran up the steep

Lowell on his horse, Lightning, at the old homeplace

hill and immediately began nuzzling him. The photos don't do justice to her size, but let's just say she's a big'un!

Lowell said that he's always loved to fish and hunt, and both sports were a big part of his early life. He said, "When we lived in the red house and it would rain, we couldn't work the corn, and Daddy would say, 'You boys can go fishing because it's too wet to hoe.' Back then, we loved to hand fish in the streams for native trout over on Nettle Creek or Irish Creek."

When I asked how hand fishing was done, Lowell explained. "Fish would go under a rock, and you'd have to stick your hand under there to git him. The trick was to squeeze him tight when you got ahold of him and bring him on out. We'd catch a bunch in this fashion and then go home and have a big fish fry." I wanted to know if the fish would ever slide out of their hands when they grabbed him, and Lowell laughed and replied, "We wouldn't *let* him!"

Hunting was another favorite sport that Lowell could never get enough of. He tells about how he started out. "There wasn't

Lowell with his draft horse, Pocahontas

too many deer back then, so in 1952, we got to bear hunting. In 1954, we got a real pack of bear dogs. They was yellow and white and brindle and what they called a cur dog. There are different kinds of curs now: leopard curs, black-mouth curs, and brindles. These kinds of dogs always treed the bear. We never had to kill a bear on the ground."

I asked what some of the differences were between bear hunting back then and today. Lowell said, "We'd take a jeep

Lowell and Pocahontas

out and didn't put anybody on a stand; you just hunted with your dogs. When they hit a track, you knew the bear was going to climb. There was no 'stop' in those dogs; the more the bear fought them, the better they liked it. You could just about get [a dog] killed, and it wouldn't whup him on out. The next day he'd be right back at it.

"Back then, we didn't have no two-way radios and tracking collars. It was just you and your gun and climbing through the laurel thickets. My brother Jesse had a dog named Rowdy, and I had a female named Blaze. Blaze was the mother and grandmother of all the good dogs we ever had, and Rowdy was the daddy. He had a lot of grit and stamina to stay on the bear, and she had the nose to get up and find him. Blaze always fought at the head, and the other dogs fought from the back. Rowdy weighed about a hundred pounds and would hold right onto [a bear] until [it] would knock him away, and you'd hear Rowdy's teeth fly off the hide with a 'pop!'

"We bred our two dogs and got one named Blackie, who was one of the best dogs that was ever around here. Biggest bear I killed back at the Fletch place weighed over four hundred pounds. Jesse and Harry Fauber killed one that weighed in at 449 pounds back on Nettle Creek. Funny thing, after all that, we don't eat bear meat! L. E. and our nephew Mutt love it, and Mama could cook it so nobody could tell the difference between that and beef."

I asked, "How are things different today than back when you were growing up?"

"Everything's different," Lowell said. "You didn't go to the store to buy hardly nothing; now you can eat steak every night if you got the money. We didn't know what eating out was. You had your milk and your hog meat. Times are better, Lynn, in a way, but the people don't have the love for each other like they did when we grew up. You worked together.

"Wilson Seaman would come up and help us pull calves, you know, heifers having calves, and in turn, we'd go back and help him get up hay, and we did that until he died. Now there doesn't seem to be much fellowship with people. Back then you didn't have any way to go see your neighbor but to walk or ride a horse, and you'd stay three or four hours when you went. Now we have big Cadillac cars that can go one hundred miles an hour in just a few minutes, and we don't take time or won't take time to go and say hi to a neighbor. It's gradually getting plumb away, and we've gotten too independent ourselves, and it's going to have to quit. We're going to have to start working together again.

"I guess a whole lot of people didn't have a lot of money, even in my time. When you came to help someone, you didn't expect no money. I've heard my mother say that if a man had a whole hillside to cut off to put corn in or wheat to farm, they would have a working during the day and then a dance at night. The man would say, 'If you come and help me next Saturday, then I'll give you a dance Saturday night.' And fifty people would show up and clean the whole hillside off in one day's time. Then it would shift off, and people would help somebody else, and *they'd* give a dance. It was a way to work and have a good time all in the same day."

Right here in the conversation, Viola and Lowell both said that the little village of Montebello is still like that. Lowell said, "We've got a close connection here, and you might have to call somebody to help you, but they will always come, never expecting any money. I would have liked to seen it stayed like it was, but we're better off now than we were in one sense of saying it, but in a way we're not. When you lose that close connection with other people, you lose the main thing."

We whiled away the afternoon talking, laughing, and enjoying the coffee and chocolate cake Viola served us, never realizing that today (November 15) was her birthday! It made the visit even sweeter, and we all agreed that we'd always remember the exact date of the interview. After we ate, I popped another tape in the recorder and set Lowell loose, asking him to tell a few of his famous tales. They had us in hysterics. I know that a lot will be lost in translation because one has to actually be there to hear Lowell's voice and see his facial expressions to truly appreciate the story.

Since these stories are true, I am going to change the names of the folks in them, even though everybody around here already knows who they are. And I ask understanding from my astute copy editor, Tania Seymour, for Lowell's usage of the native mountain tongue.

Lowell and Viola today (2013)

STORIES FROM THE MOUNTAINS
As told by Lowell Humphreys

Clive Campbell was a preacher down on Irish Creek, and he got a coon dog tryin' him out to buy, and he hadn't treed no coons for Clive, and Clive had one more night before he took him back to the owner. He was talking to Rayburn Willis, who lived down on Irish Creek, and he said, "Rayburn, I got a dog I'm tryin' out but he ain't done much for me. I don't know if I'm not hunting where the coons are or what."

Rayburn said, "Son, go on up to Mary Creek. I guarantee, you go the head of Mary Creek and you'll catch a coon." So they went over there and had the dog in the trunk. Rayburn was kind of a hyper type and jumped out of the car before Clive could cut the engine off, and going down the bank he heered a coon climbing a pine tree, bark falling. He never told Clive about it, and Clive turned the dog out, and the old dog went down in the creek and started bawling, "boo-hoo, boo-hoo," ducking down the creek, and come back to him directly and shook the water off hisself.

Rayburn said, "Clive, son, that dog no good . . . put him back in the trunk. I smell that coon myself, and I'm gonna tree him for ya."

Clive said, "Aww, Rayburn what you talkin' 'bout?"

Rayburn shot back, "Put him in the trunk so he don't mess that track up nowhere." Then Rayburn commenced to run down the creek bawling, "boo-hoo, boo-hoo."

Directly Clive yelled, "Come out, Rayburn, I'm going to leave you if you don't."

"It's all right son, I'm going to git him straightway, the track's getting' hot now." Rayburn walked up to that tree and put his hand on it and barked like a dog, yelling to Clive, "Go in there and throw that light up and see if he ain't in there." When Clive hesitated, Rayburn yelled again, "Clive, throw that light in there. I smell his track up this tree."

Clive did and said, "I hope to die, there he sits!"

Rayburn said, "Shoot him out, son, shoot him out!" Rayburn told folks from then on, "I never did tell Clive I didn't smell the coon track, and I heard him climbing up that tree."

John was just a boy, like, and uncle Henry's brother, Josh, was eighteen months younger than John and had a gray stud work colt and kept him in the barn and carried water to him and fed him corn and hay, and the colt felt so good, he was just a squealing and kicking in that barn. They didn't ride him, never brought him out.

Uncle Josh said, "I'm going to ride ol' Robie up to the water today. I ain't going to carry no water; he's going to drink out of the creek today." He

Lowell telling one of his stories

got on him, and that ol' horse throwed Uncle Josh. They got him back in the barn, and Uncle Josh told little John to take all the big floppy hats that the aunts and grandma were terrible about ordering from the catalog and send them back because they didn't fit. He told John, "Take an old hen, son, and go down to the post office and sell the hen and take the money and use it for postage and send them old hats back."

Well, suh, [John] got on that gray colt, riding him down there, and was doing right good until the old hen flopped. It scared that colt, and while [John] had ahold of the hen and the hats, the colt jumped out from under him, and John threw the hen and the hats in the creek, and the colt ran off home in front of him.

They put the colt back in the barn, and, in a day or two, when it was a pretty fall day, John's grandpa told Uncle Josh, "Josh, go get that colt and put a saddle on him because I'm gonna break him for you all boys. I rode in the cavalry and ain't never been throwed. I'm going to break him this morning."

Uncle Josh put the saddle on him, and Grandpa climbs on and tells [Josh] to go cut some switches off a big chestnut tree where the colt was standing and says he's going to whip the orneriness out of him. The colt was a stud horse, and he wanted to go one way and Grandpa wanted him to go the other, so he was balky.

Little John said, "Grandpa, what you want me to do?"

Grandpa yelled, "You little devil, you get on in the house and don't you come out."

This hurt John's feelings and he thought to himself, "Old man, if that's how you feel about it, that's what I'll do!" On his way to the house, he spied a big ol' chestnut burr busted open, and as he went by the colt, he eased the burr up under his tail and that colt jumped off the ground and started squealing and kicking and bucking. He said he never saw nothing to beat it in his life.

The colt reared up on his hind feet, and the old man lost his hat. When he come down, his false teeth flew out on the ground. The colt was whirling and kicking, whirling and kicking. Uncle Josh got over behind a rock and said, "That colt's going to kill Grandpa."

"No," says little John, "he's been in the cavalry and he's gonna ride him . . . he's gonna stick with him!"

The colt raised up high on his hind feet and the saddle girth busted and fell down around his feet. He kicked the saddle and Grandpa right over there with the boys behind the rock. Grandpa noticed that the colt kept on kicking and bucking with nothing on him but the bridle.

Grandpa hollered, "Hey, you fool you, if I had a pistol, I'd shoot you!"

After a while, the horse got all in a lather and it tickled little John to death. Nobody knew he had slipped that burr under the horse's tail. All at once, that colt quite bucking and pulled hisself up in a knot and lifted his tail and let that chestnut burr fall out. John took out running and Grandpa threw two rocks at him that if they hit, would have killed him. Just to be on the safe side, for a few days John ate supper long after his grandpa went to bed at night. But after that, whenever they saddled up the colt to ride, he never bucked again. It sure enough broke him.

Martha Ramsey and Mary Wright

4

Mary Bridge Wright and Martha Bridge Ramsey

I first met Mary Wright thirty-three years ago when we were both going to the Mennonite Church at the bottom of the mountain where I live. Mary was a member of the large Bridge family, and Mountain View Mennonite Church is where the majority of her siblings also attended. Sometime along the way, I met her twin sister, Martha Ramsey, whose husband, Charles, was the minister at Stuarts Draft Mennonite Church. I was immediately drawn to these ladies because of their warm and nurturing personalities and the way they always made me feel welcome. My first impression of them has proved true all these years later, so I was delighted when they agreed to let me interview them for *Appalachian Heart*.

We spent a very enjoyable afternoon talking and looking through old photographs, which they generously lent me for their chapter of the book. Notice that from the earliest of these photos right up to the present time, Mary and Martha have always dressed alike and were—and still are—beautiful women. I am now pleased to be able to write their beautiful story as well.

Their grandparents on their paternal side were Jesse and Bettie Treavy Bridge; on the maternal side were Isabelle Henderson and her first husband Gilbert Lowery (Isabelle later married Ed Brydge). Mary and Martha's father, Junius ("Junie") Blair Bridge, was the son of Jesse and Bettie; their mother, Lonie Evelyn Lowery, was the daughter of Gilbert and Isabelle. The Jesse Bridge family lived in a log cabin just down the road from the conjunction of Reed's Gap and Love Road.

The Jesse Bridge family (1907); Junie is at the very back holding the banjo

Junie and Lonie courted, married on September 10, 1911, and continued to live in the same home where Junie was raised, and, in turn, he and Lonie raised their large family there. Fourteen children were born to the Bridges, and the order of their births are as follows: Ruth, 1912; Hazel Mae, 1913; Hershel, 1915; Rachel, 1917; Thelma, 1920; Junius (Leslie), 1922; Jesse, 1924; Reginald, 1926; Dorothy, 1928; Naomi, 1931; Mary and Martha, July 1, 1933; and another set of twins, Benjamin and Joseph, January 18, 1935.

Hazel Mae died in 1915 at two years of age; Thelma died in 1925 at five years of age; and Benjamin only lived for a month, passing away on February 13, 1935. It is thought that severe diarrhea, which was called the bloody flux back then, was responsible for a couple of the deaths. Mary and Martha's brother Jesse once told me that either Hazel Mae or Thelma died from burns when her skirt caught fire from the flames under an outside wash kettle.

Junie and Lonie, at far right, before marriage (1909)

Ed and Isabelle Brydge with baby Paul and Junie and Lonie Bridge (1909)

He told the story of the little girl crying, "Blow, Mama, blow," asking her mother to cool her burning skin with her breath. The eleven Bridge children remaining lived to adulthood and were as closeknit as a family can be. Of these eleven siblings, only four are left: Dorothy, Naomi, Mary, and Martha.

When asked which of the twins was born first, Mary jumped right in and said, "Martha!" After a few long seconds and a sisterly "look,"

Martha quietly explained, "Mary was born four hours before I was. Mama went into a coma after Mary was born, and someone went and got Doctor Morton and brought him back to the house. Back then, you didn't know if there were two babies coming or

Martha and Mary (c. 1937)

not. I'm not sure if I was breech, but Doctor Morton finally delivered me and Mama came to and was all right after that. Eighteen months later, she had another set of twins, Joseph and Benjamin."

Junie Bridge was a farmer, growing most everything his large family needed to be self-sufficient, but he also cut timber and owned and operated a general mercantile store just down the road from their home that sold gasoline. Mary and Martha were small at the time, but they can still remember going to the store and their daddy giving them each a piece of candy. They also recall his generosity to the local people, giving them credit when they didn't have the money to pay their bill until the next paycheck. When a person came in with a list of things she needed, Junie would be the one to get the items, ring them up, and bag or box the purchase. It was the same with gasoline; those were the days before self-service everything!

The store later burned down, but Junie continued to buy large bags of flour, beans, salt, and sugar from the farm bureau wholesale house in Staunton, then sell them to people out of a small building that was located at the end of their lane. A lot of folks did not have vehicles back then and came to the store in horse and wagon to take their purchases home. Junie also raised chickens for the Weaver Hatchery in Stuarts Draft. Mary said that at one time, he had chicken houses that could accommodate three thousand chickens at a time.

Junie Bridge's mercantile store

Martha added that her daddy helped to build the Skyline Drive (what mountain people called the Blue Ridge Parkway). He would walk from their homeplace each morning to where they were constructing the road. Their brother Jesse told the girls that when he was a boy, their mama would pack her husband's supper and send Jesse up the mountain to take it to him. Martha said that was the only public paying job their daddy ever had.

Both girls also helped when their father was cutting logs to sell. "If Daddy was cutting logs on the Drawbond place [property that adjoined

From left to right:
Anna Willis, Martha, and Mary (1944)

Bridge land], Mary and I would ride the horse and pull the logs out for him," recalled Martha. She said that sometimes the chains holding the logs would twist and scare the horse and make him run off, which would frighten the girls to death. They also cut firewood with a crosscut saw and walked through the mountains picking wild blackberries that their mother would can. They sold a lot of the berries to people in West Virginia, packing them in lard cans and shipping them from the Lyndhurst train station.

Mary and Martha both remember their daddy piling dried corn shucks on a ground sled and bringing them back to the house, where they would help twist the dried kernels off the cob with their hands. Junie would then take the grain to the mill in Greenville to have it ground into cornmeal, which was a common staple in the mountain people's diet.

Their mother would rise early to make a fire in her wood-burning cookstove in the kitchen and call to the children sleeping upstairs with her familiar, "Breakfast is ready." The girls said that Lonie fixed the same breakfast every day of her life: hoecake bread, gravy, eggs, side-meat bacon, and homemade jelly.

The Bridge family kept workhorses, chickens for meat and eggs, cows for milk, and hogs for fall butchering. Martha said that in later years, they had an old Ford car that the boys would jack up. They'd put a belt on one of the wheels to run a sawmill. Sometime in the late 1940s, they put electricity in the house, and it is thought that a spark from the wiring caused a fire that destroyed the entire home the morning of February 20, 1950.

Mary said, "No one was at home at the time except Mama. The younger children were at school, the older ones were working, and Daddy was visiting his sister Lizzie in Roanoke, who was sick. At the time, they were macadamizing [paving] the road out front and some of the workers saw the smoke and came to see about it. Mama had gone to the henhouse to gather the eggs, and when she came back, she saw the house was on fire. The only two things saved were our grandmother's rocking chair and Mama's old Maytag wringer washing machine that was on the back porch."

The family stayed with relatives that night then went to live in the Ed and Isabelle Brydge home for a year until a new house could be built. Mary said that up until that time, their mother had always made their clothes out of printed chicken feed sacks, but when the fire broke out, their cousin Bedie Coffey, who lived in Staunton, called and told them to come up because she wanted to buy them some new clothes. Those were the first store-bought clothes they'd ever had, and both remember the brown corduroy skirts, red sweaters, and the other things that their cousin bought them.

Junie and Lonie Bridge in 1949 before the house burned down

I had always assumed that the Bridge family had belonged to the Mennonite church right from the beginning, but I was surprised to learn that they had not become members of that faith until a later time, when they began attending Mountain View Church. Up to that time, the family had worshipped at the Dunkard (Brethren) church, located up the mountain in Love, or the Methodist church in Sherando.

The older Bridge children went either to the early Laurel Hill School, located on a flat across from Mountain View Church, or walked up the mountain to the Snead School in Love. Both of those schools were closed by the time Mary and Martha were old enough to go to the first grade, so they attended the Sherando Elementary School, which had grades one to five. They went to the sixth grade at Stuarts Draft School, the seventh at a one-room Mennonite school located close to the Lyndhurst train depot

Martha and Mary's 1951 school photo

where Bessie Hailey taught, and later to the Augusta Mennonite School near Stuarts Draft before finishing up their junior and senior years at Wilson Memorial in Fishersville. They graduated in 1951, a month before their eighteenth birthday.

After graduation, the twins both got jobs at Roses Dime Store in Waynesboro, and their older brother Jesse took them to work. He also let them borrow his car to go out and have a little fun. Mary met and started to date her future husband, Don Wright, while working at the dime store. Both girls had started courting boys during their senior year, but their mother had always told them that "boys and books don't go

Mary and Martha's 1951 graduation photos

together," so they had to sneak out and go to their older married sister's house to meet their dates.

Later, different boys would come to their home to pick them up, and Mary said that her daddy and mama were okay with that. They went to square dances, movies, bowling, and roller skating or just rode around and had a good time, but the twins said that they had been raised to know right from wrong and never did anything that would hurt their parents.

Left to right: Charles and Martha, Mary and Don (1955)

Everyone was expected to get up on Sunday morning to go to church. Mary said, "You would have to be sick or have a good reason if you didn't go to church. And we *wanted* to go." Although each of the girls dated a good bit before marriage, they said that they were ready to settle down when the time came.

Both girls left their jobs at Roses and found work as attendants at Western State Hospital. They stayed in those jobs for about a year before finding employment at the DuPont Plant in Waynesboro. This was around 1953, and Mary helped line up a blind date for her sister with a co-worker's brother, Charles Ramsey. At the time, Charles was in the Air Force, but after two years of service, he came home to stay. The girls dated their future husbands for a number of years before they set the date for their weddings. By this time, they were all working at the General Electric Company, which later became Genicom, in Waynesboro. Both Don and Charles retired from this company after many years of service. Mary and Martha worked until each had her first child, then they became full-time mothers.

Don and Mary Wright on their wedding day (July 14, 1956)

Mary married Don at Mountain View Mennonite Church on July 14, 1956. The newlyweds moved in with Mary's parents for a short while until they found an apartment in Waynesboro, but they only stayed there for six weeks before buying a little home on Delphine Avenue. Their first son, Ronnie, was born while living at this residence. Mary was pregnant with her daughter Donna when they moved to a home they'd built in Sherando on five acres of land they had bought. Donna, her sister Phyllis, and brother D. F. were born at this home, where the Wrights continue to live. In 2006,

*Mary and Don with their children (Ronnie, D. F., Phyllis, and Donna)
on their fiftieth wedding anniversary*

Mary and Don celebrated their fiftieth wedding anniversary, and this year will make fifty-seven years since they said their vows and became husband and wife. In addition to their four children, the Wrights now have ten grandchildren.

Martha married Charles at Mountain View one year later on July 13, 1957. After marriage, the Ramseys lived in several apartments in Waynesboro before buying their first home in Stuarts Draft. Two of their four children (Doug and Cindy) were born while the couple lived at their Stuart Avenue home. They later sold this house and moved in with Martha's brother Leslie while a new home was

*Charles and Martha Ramsey on their wedding day
(July 13, 1957)*

being built in Sherando, where they had purchased thirty-five acres of land. Their last two children (Mark and Tony) were born while they were living in this home, where the Ramseys continue to reside. The Ramseys celebrated their fiftieth anniversary in 2007, and this year will mark their fifty-sixth milestone of marriage. They now have eight grandchildren and two great-grandchildren.

Martha and Charles with their children (Doug, Cindy, Tony, and Mark)
on their fiftieth wedding anniversary

The twins learned to tack quilts at an early age, and in 1991, Mary and Martha hand stitched a beautiful quilt hanging for their fortieth class reunion at Wilson Memorial High School in honor of the 1951 graduating class. The sisters designed the unique quilt in the Cathedral Window pattern, and it has each of the 224 class members' names cross-stitched inside the individual "windows." The larger center panel has a hornet's nest stitched on it, which is Wilson's school logo—the Green Hornets. The hanging was sewn in green and white, which continue to be the school colors sixty-two years later.

The quilt has been on display at each annual reunion since 1991, and every year it is updated to include tiny black crosses on

Martha and Mary with the school quilt they made

the windows of former classmates who have passed away during the year. School reunions can be one of the most rewarding times of a person's life as classmates return to their alma mater to recall fond memories and to learn more about the people with whom they spent their high school years.

I had to ask about the stories of twins being on the same wavelength—physically and mentally—and Mary and Martha confirmed that there is something to it. Many times, when one is in pain, the other feels it, even though she may not be aware that her sister is hurting at the time. Martha laughs when she says, "One time, Mary's back was bothering her, and I said, 'I sure hope you feel better, so I can too!'" They also say that many times their thoughts seem to run in the same direction. And from childhood until the present, the twins continue to dress alike most of the time. Looking over the photographs in this chapter, you can see that statement is true.

The Bridge family was close-knit, and all the siblings helped one another throughout their lives. Speaking about their mother, the sisters said that she was a hard worker and always had a gentle

Martha and Mary in 2003   *Martha and Mary in 2013*

spirit; they never remember a time when she was mad or upset. They also said that their dad was gentle with all the children and never had to discipline them harshly. Martha said that he had a certain "look" he gave them, and they knew that whatever he asked, they had better get to it!

"We had such kind and loving parents," Martha said, "and I never heard them say one unkind word to each other; even with having all us children, they had the patience of Job. We had all these cousins coming over, and now we have our houses all fixed just so and don't want them torn up, but back then our parents let us play and never told us to wipe our feet or not to touch anything."

The Bridge children were taught to be kind to one another, and Mary and Martha said that the siblings were not ever allowed to hit one another. Their dad always said that if anybody did the hitting, it would be him. All the siblings worked hard for their own families and others as well. Wherever there was a need, the twins said that they tried to fill it. They always made sure that someone in the family or a hired woman stayed with their mother each night after their dad passed away in 1963, and they took turns cleaning their mother's house and doing her washing until she died in 1977. They did the same for their brother Jesse, who

Junie (far right) and Lonie (far left) Bridge with their eleven children

continued to live in the family homeplace until he passed away in October 2012.

When asked if they thought living was better back when they were growing up or in today's world, both agreed that the old times were wonderful in some ways, but they are thankful every day that they have warm homes to live in, washers and dryers to do their laundry, and all the conveniences that modern-day living affords.

Mary summed it up with her last statement: "We are the most blessed people in the world, and I tell people this really often. As a big family to be raised up in the mountains, we were taught to work, and we loved to work. We had the best parents, who taught us right, and had a church right up the road that we could attend. To have a family that willingly takes care of us when we need help makes all the difference in the world."

Ted Hughes with one of his restored surreys

5

Ted Hughes

We met Ted and his wife, Jane, in 2008 when Ted's younger cousin (also a Ted Hughes) invited Billy and me to a Christmas open house held at the old Proffitt Mill on Warwick Barn Road in Amherst County, Virginia. The E. M. Proffitt & Son Grist Mill and General Merchandise Store (circa 1910) originally belonged to Jane's family, but it had closed and fallen into disrepair. Ted and Jane bought the old

Proffitt's Mill, restored

building, that also housed a blacksmith shop in the early days, and in 2007 the mill was restored by the Hughes family. The following Christmas season, it was opened to the public and had displays of antique tools and equipment, as well as grinding demonstrations given by Ted in the old mill.

Sign on the restored building

Jane had decorated the interior in holiday style; a spread of delicious finger foods and handmade gifts available for purchase were laid out on tables. I bought an old lantern filled with candy and gave it as a Christmas gift to one of our neighbors.

After that initial open-house meeting, Billy and I received invitations to come visit the Hughes's business, the Chalk Level Carriage & Buggy Works. I was sorry I hadn't known about Ted's special talent

Cornmeal being ground in the mill

for restoring all types of horse-drawn vehicles and equipment when I was still publishing *Backroads*. Since the content of the three Backroads books came directly from the old newspaper articles, Ted's unique business was never featured in them, either. When the decision was made to publish *Appalachian Heart*, I knew immediately that I wanted to include the Hugheses. So sit back and get ready to enjoy how the Chalk Level Carriage & Buggy Works came to be.

Ted's parents, Lewis and Pauline Hughes

Ted was the middle child of three children born to Lewis Hughes and his wife, Pauline Wilson Wood Hughes, who married in 1926 and lived in Massies Mill. Ted came into the world on September 18, 1935, and there were eight years between him and his older brother, Lewis, born in 1927, and younger sister, Betty Ann, born in 1943.

Lewis, Sr., grew up in Rhue Hollow, and all his close relatives lived in the Rockfish Valley area of Nelson County, Virginia. Five generations back, Ted's fifth great-grandfather was awarded four land grants in Nelson County and one 45,000-acre grant in Kentucky for his Revolutionary War service. The large tract of land in Kentucky was awarded to both him and Alexander Reid, who is the man that Reid's Gap and Reid's Creek were named after.

Pauline's people were from the Massies Mill area, and, at one time, they lived in the large home, called Three Springs, owned by the Congers family. Ted and his siblings were born and raised right in the heart of Massies Mill in a large home that was once a boarding house run by Henry Parrish. The house boasted running water and a bathroom that Mr. Parrish had installed before the Hugheses moved there.

Henry and Ivetta Parrish and family at the boarding house where Ted's family lived

Ted said that a large spring was located on the mountain across the Tye River, and a waterline was run to Grace Episcopal Church, Lea's Store, the bank, the Mahone's house, and their home. When asked about hot water, Ted said that his mother had a Home Comfort wood-burning cookstove. It had a large water reservoir on the back that was heated by the stove, then the water was piped to the bath by gravity.

Ted's father worked at Lea Brothers' Store, located next to their house, and his day began at six o'clock in the morning when he walked next door to open up. At seven, the farm hands arrived, and Lewis would leave with them to go work in the orchards or the large farm that the Lea's also owned. When the day's work was done and the hands went home, Lewis went back to the store and worked until dark.

On Saturday nights, the store remained open until eleven at night, and, although it was closed on Sunday, the cows still needed to be milked and the cattle fed, so it was hardly a day of rest. Lewis got two days off each year—Thanksgiving and Christmas—but on Thanksgiving day, the family butchered their hogs, and on Christmas day, they cut firewood, so he didn't get to enjoy the relaxing holiday season that we are accustomed to nowadays.

Ted recalls that Massies Mill was a real boom town when he was young. "There was the Fleetwood School that had grades one through eleven; the Coffey's had a cider mill, store, and sawmill on one side of the bridge; Higgs and Young Company made wooden barrels and baskets used in the apple orchards; the DePriest Bank was inside Lea's Store at first and later moved across the road into its own building, but it was closed when I was young. The post office for Massies Mill was also located inside Lea Brothers' Store, and my mother was the postmistress there for many years. She got an hour

Ted as a toddler with his dog, Spot (the walnut tree to the right of Ted's head still stands)

for lunch and walked home to cook a hot meal in the middle of the day, in addition to breakfast and supper.

"There was a cooper shop, Reynolds's Shoe Shop, Mahone's Store, Thomas Ligon's saw mill, Charlie Higginbottom's store, Wallace Smith had a restaurant and beer joint. Massie's Mill was still grinding back then and was owned by L. W. Meeks. When he died, Elwood Jones inherited it and later Mrs. Morton bought it. It was still in operation at the start of World War II.

"There were two active churches in Massies Mill: Grace Episcopal and the Presbyterian Church, which was destroyed by Hurricane Camille and later rebuilt across the main road from where it once stood. There were two blacksmith shops, and people would bring their horses into town to be shod. One man brought a huge workhorse into the blacksmith shop and put his head in the stock, and when the horse raised his head, he picked up the whole stock and started down through town carrying it.

"In the early years, my mother played the player piano for a theater that showed silent movies. The theater, owned by Mr. Smith, later burned down. There was a train depot across the road from where the Lea Brothers' had a long wooden building where they sold orchard sprays (now owned by Dickie Brothers at Routes 56 and 666). At that time, there were no passenger cars, but if a person wanted to ride the train, they could sit in the caboose. In town, there was a building of some kind on every lot, and the outlying areas were all farmland."

Massies Mill (1915–16)

Massies Mill looking north from Grace Church (1919)

Ted attended Fleetwood and walked to school in the early days, but later he rode the busses that Jim Redd, Dennett Hughes,

Withers Ponton, and Hawes Parrish drove. Children from the Campbell, Mahone, Powell, Miller, Johnson, Ponton, Napier, and Hughes families also went to school with Ted at Fleetwood. Ted got his driver's license when he was fifteen years old, and his daddy bought him his first car: a 1946 Crosley. At fifteen, Ted also got his Social Security card because he went to school for half a day, then worked the other half measuring tobacco allotments.

At this point in our conversation, I began asking Ted's wife, Jane, about her family. Her parents were Chester Proffitt and Lois Cash Proffitt. Her mother was raised over by Turkey Mountain, and her father's people settled along Warwick Barn Road, where she and Ted continue to live. Jane's grandfather ran a mill that was restored in 2007 (see the photos at the beginning of this chapter), and it is located a little farther down on Warwick Barn Road.

Jane said that her parents may have known each other when they were younger, but it wasn't until her father came home from service that they took notice of each other more seriously. Or, as Jane put it, "He saw her and she saw him, and that was it!"

Jane was born in 1936 and has one sister, Fay. She says of her and Ted's birthdays, "For six months, we are the same age, and for the other six months, Ted is older." Asked if they'd grown up together, Jane said that she attended the Temperance School in Amherst County, while Ted went to Fleetwood. "Back then, if you didn't go to the same school or church together, you didn't get a chance to meet."

How they did meet was at a dance in Lovingston when Jane was older and enrolled in Phillips Business College, attending secretarial classes. Ted had gone to the same school to study accounting—work he never did go into. At the dance, Ted came up to Jane; making conversation, he casually asked, "You go to Phillips Business College, don't you?" When she replied affirmatively, Ted became bolder and said, "You're having [another] dance soon, aren't you. Why don't you ask me?" The rest, as they say, is history.

They began dating, then married at Central Baptist Church in a large traditional wedding on August 6, 1955. The newlyweds honeymooned in Williamsburg, and both laughed at the memory of not having ten dollars between them. Ted said that was back when gasoline was twenty cents a gallon and groceries were cheap. "But we still were living hand to mouth," he recalled.

The couple set up housekeeping in a four-room home where they continue to live. Jane's dad had a garage that had burnt down on the property, and he had built a home for a widowed aunt on the same foundation. When the aunt remarried and moved away, Jane's parents gave the house to the newly married couple. Over the years, Ted put his carpentry skills to work and built seven more rooms onto the house. It is cozy, yet open and airy, inviting warm conversation around the dining room table where we sat during the interview.

Before the Chalk Level Carriage & Buggy Works was formally opened as a business, Jane had retired from Contel Telephone Company after twenty-five years of service, and Ted had retired from VDOT. Ted had always had a knack for fixing things, but his first formal repair of a horse-drawn vehicle came when he and Jane were in a horse-riding and driving club, and someone needed their wagon repaired. As Jane said, "Mr. Handyman took care of it!" A little while later, the same person had a buggy that needed some work done, and Ted agreed to repair it.

On their anniversary, Ted and Jane took a day off and drove to Buena Vista. There they saw an old surrey standing outside a general store and inquired about buying it from the owner. A tree had grown up through the center of the surrey, and it was not in good condition. But a deal was struck, and soon the vehicle was on its way back to the Hughes's farm. Ted started working on the surrey. When it was finished, someone from the newspaper did an article on it. It wasn't long after that an undertaker who had seen the story called to ask if Ted would consider restoring an old hearse. Things just started branching out, and more people began calling.

In November 1991, the Hugheses had their first open house, held outdoors and with three horse-drawn vehicles on display. Jane said, "We had three pieces of restored equipment, and two people attended the open house. Well, you've got to start somewhere!"

I asked about the unique name they had chosen for their business; Jane said it was descriptive of the type of soil they have in their area. She also said that it has been told in years past that there was an old plantation by that name standing on the same site, but she cannot document it as fact.

Ted already had a twenty-four by forty foot building on the property where he put the farm equipment he was working on. The building was later expanded to house the ever-growing number of

The Chalk Level Buggy Works

restoration pieces that came in. When asked how many pieces he's finished, Ted scratched his head, conferred with Jane, and they both agreed that the number is in the hundreds. Ted has restored a total of twenty-eight antique carriages, sleighs, and buggies just for the Robert Thomas Carriage Museum in the town of Blackstone, Virginia. He has restored mail wagons, a vis-à-vis carriage, a Victoria, a French cabriolet, a Cuban Valente, a Sicilian donkey cart, a water buffalo cart from Siam, several cannons and caissons, a multitude of sleighs, an English tub cart, reapers, two Civil War wagons, an omnibus, wagonettes, three adult hearses, one child's white hearse, and a street sweeper from Cincinnati, Ohio.

He also completely built from scratch a Civil War ambulance. Ted said he had done seven or eight pieces for a man who also wanted an 1860s ambulance. The only pieces Ted didn't make for the vehicle were the wheels and the springs. Ted ordered the specifications for an Army wagon from Fort Lee, then he and Jane were invited to come to take pictures and go behind the scenes to look at the ambulances in the quartermaster museum. The plans called for pine and walnut wood, but the man ordering the vehicle wanted the whole thing made out of solid cherry, which was milled at Mike Ramsey's saw mill. Fifty pounds of horse hair at twelve dollars a pound was ordered out of Ohio to stuff the seats.

When finished, the ambulance could carry eight wounded soldiers who were still able to stand (four on each side); if the men had been seriously wounded, it could carry four—two on the top stretchers and two on the seats below. Ted also mounted two wooden casks on the vehicle: one for water, the other for whiskey, which was used as a pain killer for the wounded. Ted said he put in two to three hundred hours of labor on the vehicle, and it was in the shop for more than a year. At the 2011 open house, I remember seeing the finished ambulance, and it truly was a work of art.

The only non-horse-drawn vehicle that Ted has undertaken to restore is the one currently in his shop. It is a 1924 Double T Ford truck, and Ted explained that it was the biggest truck Ford made at the time. The cab and body were kept in a garage in Amherst County and is owned by Doris Moses of Charleston, West Virginia. The truck had at one time belonged to her uncle. She wants the old vehicle restored because it was in her family, and she wants to keep it in the family. Ted says that he should have it finished by the next open house held in November 2013.

Although Jane does not help her husband with the restorations, Ted gives her much praise for keeping the books and taking care of the money that comes in. "That's the reason we've got what we've got now," he said. "If it was up to me, I'd buy everything I see!"

In the past, Ted has taken several of his finished pieces, such as the hearses and fancy surreys, and hired them out at funerals and weddings for people wishing to add an old-time touch. With a matched team of horses in harness pulling the vehicles, it is an impressive sight.

The year Ted retired, he built a covered wagon. He and a buddy went to Lynchburg when the bateau festival started and followed the boats down the James River on the roads snaking alongside. They drove 108 miles that week en route to Richmond, where

The early stages of a hearse restoration

The hearse under construction

the river boats finished their run. The men took enough food for themselves and the horses and would camp where the people on the bateaus stopped for the night.

The hearse restoration completed

A surrey before Ted began restoration

Ted and Jane were also avid equestrians. They belonged to a riding club and helped establish the Montebello trail ride held each spring and fall. In fact, Ted told me that one year, he and

Completed surrey ready for a wedding party

good friend Tony Leebrick of Lowesville spent the weekend at the Montebello ride. Instead of taking their animals by trailer to Montebello, they decided to ride the horses across the mountain, up Shoe Creek, and over to the base camp at the firehouse where the trail ride was to be held. He laughed and said that by the time they had ridden all the way up the mountain, spent two days riding trails, then ridden all the way home, he could hardly walk for several days afterward!

The couple also belonged to two local western square dance clubs: the Blue Ridge Stars and Grand Squares of Nelson. They were active in both for twenty-five years, dancing at least twice a week. They danced at festivals and conventions, served on convention committees, and danced at the national competitions held in Baltimore, where there were ten thousand people dancing at one time. In the last two years, because of back problems, Ted hasn't been able to participate, but Jane continues to go to classes at least once a week and to the club dances held in Amherst. She goes alone and says that club members always make sure the "loose women" have a chance to dance with a partner. She says that square dancing allowed them to make friends with folks they would not have otherwise met and maintains that they are "friendships set to music where you can't find a nicer bunch of people!"

The Hugheses have had a happy life together and celebrated their fifty-seventh wedding anniversary in August 2012. They have two daughters: Paula and Susan. Paula and her husband, Jim, have two sons and live in Charlottesville. Susan and her husband, Roger, have one daughter and live directly to the rear of the Buggy Works. Susan and Roger have their own business, Maple Run Woodworks, where they make fine furniture and cabinetry and do picture framing.

Jane and Ted Hughes at their 2012 open house

As we wound up the interview, I asked Ted if he had one favorite piece from all those he has restored. He admitted that each one holds a special place in his heart, and all were a challenge. At the time of this writing, the Hugheses have several sleighs, two carts, and two beautiful surreys in their shop for sale. Each piece is a thing of beauty and must be seen to be appreciated. If you are interested in talking to Ted about restoring an antique of your own or perhaps purchasing one of his, you may call him at 434-277-5166 to set up an appointment to visit the Chalk Level Carriage & Buggy Works. You will find Ted and Jane easy to talk to and a pleasure to deal with, and their work on restored antique pieces is impeccable!

Daniel Shortridge and his mule, Gus (Coffeytown)

Agnes Thompson

6

Agnes Duncan Thompson

I'm not exactly sure where Agnes and I first met. Seems she was always at the places and with the people I was covering for the *Backroads* newspaper through the years. I never had the pleasure of interviewing just her and her alone, so I wanted to include her life story within the pages of *Appalachian Heart*.

At eighty years of age, Agnes is one of the youngest people in the book. As we talked, I noticed subtle differences in her early growing up experiences in the Beech Grove community as compared to those of the elder mountain people living in areas located deeper in the mountains. The day we talked, Theresa Harris, one of Agnes's younger cousins, came over and joined us for an impromptu lunch before we settled down and began the interview.

Tubs of vintage photographs, wills, and other documents were brought out, and suddenly many generations of Agnes's family unfolded before us. Like everyone else who was interviewed for this book, Agnes trusted me to make copies of her treasured photos so that you readers could put faces with the names she talked about. Many thanks to this special woman for her warmth, humor, and willingness to share her early memories of growing up in Beech Grove, the community nestled in the shadow of Three Ridges Mountain.

Agnes's paternal grandparents were Bernard Jellette Duncan and his wife, Mary Kate Matthews Duncan. Her maternal grandparents were Lewis Forest Hughes and Susie Higginbotham Hughes, whose family was from across Brent's mountain. Agnes was told that when Susie was young, she played the organ at Jonesboro Baptist Church.

Agnes's parents were John Pearson Duncan and Ada Hughes Duncan. At this point in our talk, Agnes opened her grand-

mother Duncan's huge bible where all the names and important dates for the family were written. Mary Kate was very precise, and I marveled at her beautiful handwriting. She had meticulously recorded each event in detail, such as her son's birth: "John Pearson Duncan, born February 21, 1899, at 8:00 o'clock Tuesday morning." Agnes's mother, Ada Hughes, was born in 1912 at Heard's.

When Agnes was a child, the Duncans lived in the Adial area of Nelson County. She recalls that as you walked into the house, there was a staircase that went straight up from the front door; at the top of the steps hung two large framed photographs of her grandfather and grand-

Lewis and Susie Hughes with Ada (Agnes's mother) as an infant

mother Duncan when they were young. Agnes pointed to the old portrait of her grandmother that now graces her home, then pulled out a snapshot of her in later years. She laughingly said, "That's what age does to you!"

Standing (left to right): Pearson Duncan, Alice Duncan Sandidge,
Bernard Jellette Duncan; seated: James Brown Duncan
holding Sheilds Carter (his great-grandson)

In 1928, Agnes's dad, known by his middle name Pearson, was the mail carrier for the star route, which encompassed the Wintergreen, Nellysford, Greenfield, Avon, and Afton communities. The first and last stop on the route was at Harris's Store in Wintergreen, which was run by Mrs. Grover Harris. The mail was dropped each day at the post offices, many of which were located inside the country stores in each area. Agnes's cousin Theresa said that her grandmother, Florence Hughes Collins, was one of the first women to vote at Harris's store when women got the vote.

In Nellysford, the mail was dropped at Hughes's Store, which Agnes's other grandparents operated. She recalls that the store's

Agnes's father, Pearson, as a mail carrier for the Beech Grove area

upstairs loft housed coffins that were made by Mr. Jesse Truslow, and there was a hole in the ceiling with a railing around it through which the coffins could be lowered to the first floor when needed.

The Greenfield post office was run by Margaret Dameron, and the Avon store and post office was operated by Nellie Anderson. At the post office in Afton, the mail was sorted by Mr. and Mrs. Carleton Dawson and later by Guy Farrar. It was then put in a locked bag and taken down to the Afton train station, where the bag was hung on a pole and grabbed up by the passing train.

Agnes also recalled that a man by the name of Morgan was the telegraph operator at the train depot and to show how times have changed, when Herbert Higginbotham "Cubby" Hughes, Ada's brother, died in Salerno, Italy, during World War II, he was killed on January 30, 1944; the family didn't get word until April 30, 1944, when it came over the telegraph line. Pearson was delivering mail at Afton when Mr. Morgan received the sad news, and Pearson took the telegram back to his mother-in-law at the Nellysford store. Cubby's wife, Louise Stratton, was living with her mother-in-law, Susie Hughes, at the time and would meet Pearson each day as the mail was delivered to ask if there was a letter from Cubby, never knowing that he had been killed months before.

Pearson Duncan and Layman Dodd later drove the work bus that transported employees of the DuPont Corporation from Beech Grove to Waynesboro, where the company was located. The line ran three times daily; many times on the weekends, the locals would ride the bus to town, stay three hours to shop, then board the bus back home. Agnes said Layman Dodd drove the morning run at six thirty, and her dad drove the afternoon shift at two thirty. They alternated nights for the late shift, which ran at ten thirty.

The bus started out as the Wayne Bus Line, but around 1950, Pearson and Agnes's husband, John, bought the company and renamed it the Duncan/Thompson Bus Line. They picked up people in front of the store the Duncans operated and drove them to the various plants in Waynesboro, such as DuPont, Basic Witz Furniture, a lumber company, and Crompton Fabrics. In later years, when people became more affluent and had cars of their own, the bus line was discontinued.

Agnes was born at Martha Jefferson Hospital in Charlottes-ville, Virginia, on August 17, 1932; her only sibling, Marian, was born August 1, 1934. Her family lived on Moses Hughes Lane in Beech Grove, and the old home still stands.

John Pearson Duncan and Ada Hughes Duncan with baby Agnes

Other than two years in the Adial area and another two years in Lovingston, Agnes has lived her entire life in Beech Grove.

She remembers that in the early years, the road through the community was a narrow dirt road, and when someone came up in an automobile, she could tell by the noise of the engine who it was. Agnes said that there had been a little wooden bridge that one had to drive over, but later they put a culvert under the road and took the bridge out. She said that the road was paved sometime around 1973.

Agnes showed me several photos of a large plantation home called "Glen-Mary" that was owned by the Ewing family. The beautiful old home finally fell down, but the area where it sat is still referred to as Glen-Mary.

As a child, Agnes had what they called an acid stomach, and her mother took her to Dr. John Coleman Everett, who had a house and office on the outskirts of Nellysford (it is now the Mark Addy Bed-and-Breakfast Inn). Agnes said that her mother told her that the doctor would measure out some kind of white powder on a knife and give it to Agnes. She was brought in so often that Doc Everett told Ada, "You know how to measure it," and just gave them the whole bottle to take home. Agnes said she can still remember being in his office one night with the lamplight shining.

The Duncans belonged to the Rockfish Baptist Church, which was built in 1926 as a sister church to Adial Baptist Church (built 1850). Agnes's grandmother's family (the Matthews) were some of the first people to be buried in the Adial church cemetery. Adial was so far away that the congregation decided to build another church a little closer to the Nellysford/Beech Grove communities for the people who lived there. Although Agnes's father, Pearson, was a member of Adial, Agnes has gone to the Rockfish church since birth, and on the wall of her home is a framed cradle roll certificate dated June 13, 1933.

Agnes laughed and said people thought she was the meanest little devil there ever was when she was a small child. George Nelson, a black man who was the sexton of the church, used to sit in back of the Duncan family on Sundays and would say to Agnes's mother, "Miz Ada, it don't do you one bit of good to bring that child to church because she makes you lose your religion every Sunday!"

When Adial had revival, Ada would have to remember to take some water in a little jar because Agnes invariably got thirsty, and there was no water of any kind at the church. "I used to get the fidgets," Agnes said. "You ever get the fidgets? It feels like worms crawling up your legs, and I'd have to take my shoes off. Mama would get so aggravated at me. I've had them all my life and wouldn't wish them on anybody, but one time I told Mama, 'I hope before you die you have them so you know how they feel!' And you know, she did get them and finally understood why I couldn't sit still." At this point, I remarked that maybe what she had was restless leg syndrome. Without missing a beat, Agnes spat out, "It ain't nothing but the fidgets!"

When asked if the winters were harsher in years past, Agnes pulled out some pictures that were taken in 1966, showing the results of a blizzard that covered an eight-foot fence on their property. It was a week or so later before the state came to scrape the road. Thomas Campbell had a little bulldozer, and he pushed out a narrow track in the road, just wide enough for one car to go through. People would stop at Agnes's garage and look up the road to see if there were any other vehicles coming; if it was clear, they'd continue on. Agnes smiled and said, "These were the days before Wintergreen Resort, and the state didn't take care of us like they do now."

The Duncan family was living in Adial when Agnes was around five years old. She was supposed to start school that fall, but Lovingston was so far away and the bus ride so scary that Agnes cried for the first three days and the decision was made to take her out. By December of the same year, the family had moved to Lovingston, and Agnes felt better about attending school. She went to the first three grades there. Her teachers in Lovingston were a Miss Maniply and a Mrs. Williams.

Halfway through the third grade, the Duncans moved back to Beech Grove, and Agnes finished her schooling at the old Rockfish Valley School located between Nellysford and Afton, graduating

Rockfish Valley High School senior class (1949); Agnes is seated in the center of the bottom row

in 1949. Her classmates were from the Marshall, Napier, Hughes, Dodd, Campbell, Farrah, Fields, Pugh, Ward, and Fox families. Some of the teachers at Rockfish were Florrie Hughes, Juliette Boyd, Margaret Garth, Katie Witt, Emma Massie, Martha Goodwin, Beulah Fitzgerald, Mr. G. D. Lawman (who was also the principal), Mrs. Fitzpatrick, and Mrs. Zaidee Williams, who was Agnes's favorite teacher.

Agnes remembers a funny incident that happened while riding home on the bus one day. She and Harold Campbell were sitting across from each other in the window seats, throwing his hat back and forth, having the best time. All of a sudden, Agnes gave his hat a good sling and out the window it went. Harold hollered, "My hat's gone!" and Harvey Thompson, who was driving the bus, said, "Well whoever threw it out has got to go get it." Agnes said it liked to scared her to death because her mother had given strict instructions to never leave the bus once she got on it. Harold saved the day—and Agnes—by jumping out to retrieve his own hat.

Before the Rockfish Valley school opened, students went to the Beech Grove School, which was located in the forks of the road where Cub Creek and Reids Gap Road intersect. Agnes's

Beech Grove School students (late 1800s)

great-grandfather, James Jackson Hughes (born June 22, 1835), was the headmaster at the school at Beech Grove and also at

Agnes's great-grandfather, James Jackson Hughes (born June 22, 1835)

the Clineburg School for Girls, which was located just north of the Nellysford community. He was also the justice of the peace for Nelson County, Virginia, in 1895.

Neighbors living close to the Duncans back then were the Hickmans, Fields, Falls, Dodds, Collins, and Coffeys. The house up on Moses Hughes Lane where Agnes was raised was one and a half stories, and she remembers that when you walked in, there was a staircase off to the side and a hallway. At the end of the hall was what they called the "little room," where Agnes and her sister, Marian, slept as children. Off to the other side of the hallway was her parents' bedroom, which they also used as a sitting room. There was a separate dining room with one step down to the kitchen area. Upstairs was a

room they called the "plun-
der room"; Agnes said, "It's
where all the junk went,
and I miss it greatly!" There
was another bedroom on the
second floor that Agnes, in
later years, had to herself.

The surrounding property
was part of a large land grant
given to the original Moses
Hughes, who settled in the
Beech Grove area in the
early 1700s. Agnes and her
husband owned a portion
of the land where her child-

*Agnes and her sister, Marian,
having a snowball fight at their home*

hood home was located, and, today, many of her relatives, including her son J. L., grandson Phillip, and their families, live there.

Agnes grew up in the same community as a boy by the name
of John Thompson. Although he was six years older and driving
the school bus while she was still small, she remembers coming
home and telling her mama, "You know, that John Leslie Thompson drove our bus today, and he's not big enough to see over the
steering wheel!" She never thought anymore about him until her
parents began running the Duncan Grocery Store in 1948, which
they ran until the late 1970s.

The Duncan's carried most everything in the grocery line
and also horseshoes and horseshoe nails. Agnes said that the
funny thing was that they sold the horseshoes by the pound and
the nails by the piece. They never sold liquor or beer because
her mama said she didn't ever want to be a stumbling block to
anyone.

John Thompson served from 1943 to 1946 in the Navy during World War II on the ship *USS Carpellotti*. He had returned
home by the time Agnes's parents started tending the store.
Agnes was about sixteen years old at that time, and Ray Falls kept
coming around to court her sister, Marian. Ray told Agnes that

John Thompson's naval photo

John wanted to go out with her, but at first Agnes said that she didn't want to go out with him. "But he was a nice fella, so I decided I would, and that's when we began dating."

When asked where they went on dates, Agnes said that they'd go to a theater in Lovingston, or they'd grab a bite to eat at a local hot dog stand. They dated for several years, and during that time Agnes decided that she wanted to be a nurse. "Back then, women had two choices of what they wanted to be: a nurse or a schoolteacher. I thought I'd take the lesser of the two evils and go for nursing. I went over to the University of Virginia in Charlottesville and stayed one week before receiving a letter from Daddy on a Thursday, saying, 'If you don't like it down there, you come on home.' Well, I started packing my bags, and the next day John came to pick me up. That was the end of my nursing career, as far as taking care of other people. But I've done a lot of it within my own family over the years."

The couple married on December 22, 1951, on the heels of Marian and Ray Falls's wedding in July 1951. Agnes said that Rev. N. C. Coggin married them in his Lovingston home. Agnes remembers wearing a navy blue suit she had bought at the Snyder & Berman Company in Lynchburg, a blue sweater, and black shoes; John wore brown pants and a tan jacket. After the ceremony, John went to the Kilmartin Drug Store in Lovingston and purchased a beautiful silver music box that played "Jingle Bells" and gave it to his new bride. Agnes pointed to the treasured gift sitting on a shelf in her living room.

The newlyweds honeymooned using a car borrowed from Lewis Rodes. The Hudson had no heat. Agnes said they made it to Chatham, Virginia, the first night, then went on to Maxton, North Carolina, the next day.

After Agnes and John married, they lived the first year with her parents. The second year, the couple decided to build their own home just down the road. Everyone told them, "Don't go in debt, don't go in debt!" Times were hard, and the theme of the day was that people didn't want to be beholden to anybody. Regardless, they bought one acre along the Beech Grove Road from Lewis Rodes's place and hired Dorsey Allman, who lived in Staunton, to build the house using the natural stone found on the property.

Agnes and John did all the interior work themselves, and John helped with some of the outside, as well. Agnes said that they had a well outside the front of the house, and she laughed at the memory of bringing a bucket of water in the front door and throwing it out the back door. They moved into the home on December 10, 1952, and Agnes continues to reside there.

Early photo of Agnes's house

Almost four years later, in 1955, their only child, J. L., was born. Agnes recalls, "What a tale that was. [Before then,] John and

I had never had a night away from each other, [but], at that time, John was driving semi-trucks for Morton Frozen Foods. When the company sent them out on a run, you never knew when they'd be back. They had plants over in Crozet and one in Webster City, Iowa. If they got them out west, they ran them to Texas and California, until they got another load coming back east.

"Dr. Weems told me that J. L. would be born the twenty-eighth of November, and the company promised John he'd be home in time for the birth of the baby. But J. L. decided he wanted to come a little early and arrived on November fifth. John was in Wisconsin when he got word and arrived home on the same Friday that I came home with J. L. from the Waynesboro Hospital."

Agnes said that back then, they kept the mothers and babies for five days before the doctors would let them go home. While John was gone, Agnes had been staying with her parents at the store. Agnes said that when John came into her bedroom, "He looked all around and finally said, 'Well, where is he?' Like he expected him to be standing up in the corner somewhere."

As a baby, J. L. had a bad case of colic; Agnes sympathized with him because he'd cry and cry but couldn't tell her where it hurt. As the colic went on and on, Agnes began to grow weary, prompting her comment, "You wouldn't take a million dollars for the one you got, and you wouldn't give five cents for another like him!"

J. L. was raised up between his parents' house and the store that his grandparents ran just up the road. Agnes said that they went to the store every day, but one snowy afternoon she told J. L. that she didn't feel comfortable driving in the snow, and they wouldn't go that day. By this time, John had switched from driving trucks to being the dispatcher at Morton Foods, and he wasn't home yet.

Agnes said that they heated the house with coal She went out to the coal pile getting some in for the stove. When she came back in the house, J. L. was sitting on a chair pulling on his socks and shoes. Agnes asked him, "Where do you think you're going?" He told her, "I'm gettin' ready to go to the store; granddaddy's comin' to get me." At that time, the party line was still in operation, and J. L. had learned to dial 932, then hang up until his grandmother answered on the other end. Agnes shook her head and told him, "Well if you're going . . . I am, too!"

Agnes said that she can remember the first time she went to a Kroger grocery store in Waynesboro; she was around twelve years old. When she walked in and saw all those bins full of oranges, bananas, and grapes, she couldn't believe her eyes. Those types of fruit were seasonal in the mountain areas; treats given only at Christmastime. She said that the smell of oranges still brings back the memory of Christmas in her mind. The same with the fragrance of a cedar tree, which is what the family cut and brought home for the holiday. Funny how the mere smell of something can bring a flood of memories to the surface of one's mind.

When J. L. grew up, he married Cindy Fields on December 21, 1974. When I asked if they'd stayed here in Beech Grove, Agnes laughed and replied, "Why would you want to go anywhere else?" J. L. and Cindy have two sons. John Glenn and his wife, Jenny, live in Fluvanna County and have a son, John Glenn, Jr., and a daughter, Amber Dawn. Phillip and his wife, Courtney, live on Moses Hughes Lane next to his parents, and they have one son, John Parker Thompson.

Agnes's husband, John, died at sixty-four years of age after thirty-nine and a half years of marriage. She says that all the Hugheses die of one of two things: heart attack or cancer. John passed from the first. About ten years later, in 2000, Agnes started going out with Andrew Hickman, a distant cousin and a man she'd known all her life. We all got used to seeing them together, and I know they really enjoyed each other's company for the eight years they had before Andrew passed away in 2008.

Agnes prefers modern-day living to the good old days that she says weren't all that good. "Who wanted to bring in wood and carry out the chamber pot? When my sister, Marian, went to work for Dr. Woodworth in Waynesboro, he asked her what size house she had. She replied five rooms and a path. We didn't put an inside bathroom in until J. L. was two years old. Wash day was a real chore, trying to start a fire under a big black kettle and then do all the rinsing, wringing out, and hanging the clothes out to dry.

Agnes, Andrew Hickman, Donald Falls, and Marian Falls (April 2008)

"John hated hog butchering time, but it was something every-body did, and he had to help. He said the hog fat would get on their hands, and the doorknob got so slick you couldn't open it. Daddy used to say he saved every part of the hog except the squeal, and the only reason he didn't save that was he couldn't get ahold of it! I'd help Mama clean the chitlins [intestines]. We'd go down to the river and open them up and wash them clean. We'd do that for seven days, putting them in a pan of saltwater to soak. They would turn real white, and on the eighth day, she'd boil them and make a batter to fry them.

"And another thing; when we were children, it got so cold in the house when the fire would go out, we'd about freeze to death. Marian and I slept on a feather tick, and we'd bury on down and long about the time we got all warm and comfortable, the bed bugs would start biting. We'd yell, 'Mama, the bugs are biting,' and she'd come in to kill them with a fly sprayer. The next morning, she'd strip the whole bed down and scald it with boiling water. Mama was convinced that those bugs came out of the walls at night, because once people started painting with turpentine, they didn't see them anymore. But everyone had them, and there wasn't any use saying they didn't.

"People also had a good dose of head lice and the itch, too. I got the itch in high school, and Mama took me over to Doctor Kidd in Lovingston, who said I was the fourth case from Rockfish School that day, and he gave Mama some kind of salve for it. You put it all over your body the first three days and never washed it off. The fourth day, you took a bath in lye water, and you were left with these little red pimples. Mama sent me back to school the following day, saying, 'You got it down there . . . take it right on back!'

"When I think back on how my mother cooked meals and canned vegetables from the garden on top of a hot wood cook-stove in the summertime, I'm so glad those days are over and done with, and I hope I never see another good old day!"

I asked what had changed since she was growing up, and Agnes replied that the whole world has changed. But mostly, she felt that back then, families were closer, and you didn't have to watch out for your children as much as you do now. Her mother would let her walk up the lane to play with her cousins and tell her to make sure her aunt sent her home at the right time. You wouldn't dare do that nowadays. Agnes says the thing she misses most about the early days is the loved ones.

I finished up the interview by asking if she's had a good life. Agnes was very positive, saying, "A whole lot of times, life is what you make it. When John started

Agnes with cousin Ted Hughes

Agnes and her cousin Theresa Harris

driving long distances and J. L. came along and I was alone most
of the time, I cried for a month or two, but nobody else seemed to
care. I thought, 'Well, there's twenty-four hours in each day, and
you can either be sad or be happy, and most folks don't give a rip
which way it is'; so I told John, 'I'm not going to do anything ille-
gal, indecent, or immoral but if you aren't here, I'm going to make
myself just as happy as I can.' So that's what I did!"

Agnes has always been an avid reader, and the many book-
shelves in her home are testament to the fact she didn't have
much to read as a child. "Other than books checked out at the
school library, we didn't have any at home. I remember going over
to granddaddy Duncan's house and reading his old farm maga-
zines that I wasn't a bit interested in, and that's the reason I've
gone so book crazy at this stage of my life. I like murder myster-
ies, who-done-its, historical novels, and the Bible. I've taught the
adult ladies Sunday school class at my church since 1985. I've also
enjoyed crocheting and embroidery, but mostly I just love to read."

As the interview came to a close, we put on the finishing touches
by going outside and taking a few pictures for the story. I bade

Agnes today at her Beech Grove home

Agnes and Theresa goodbye, heading back up the mountain with a warm feeling in my heart, a packet of vintage photographs in my hand, and newfound knowledge about the Beech Grove community on tape. Agnes, who loves nothing more than reading an interesting book about local history, unknowingly just wrote her own. A heartfelt thanks to Agnes and all the other people featured in *Appalachian Heart* who trusted me to write their life stories, preserving them for future generations.

Montebello "town meeting": Douglas, Stevie, Steve, and Robbie Bryant; Lowell Humphreys; Billy Coffey

Glenn Allen playing his mandolin

7

Glenn Allen

For me, the best part of working on *Appalachian Heart* was sitting around the kitchen table talking with the mountain people I've known and loved all these years. Glenn and his wife, Lorine Coffey Allen, are no exception. It was a cool November day when we sat down to talk; before long, their son Gary came in and joined the conversation. Their story winds along the same path as that of relatives Buck and Lura (see chapter 11), yet there are subtle differences in shared experiences that add depth and richness to the story.

Through the years, I've watched this special couple and noticed certain traits they both possess that make them an inseparable unit. You cannot talk about one without thinking of the other. They are soft spoken and respectful of each other in word and deed, yet each has a dry sense of humor that pokes good-natured fun at the other with perfect timing.

For instance, I've always been touched at the way Glenn reaches out and takes his wife's hand whenever they walk together. When I commented on it, without missing a beat, Lorine said, "He's at the point now that he has to!" When the laughter died down, I saw the glint in their eyes telling me that they are still in love after sixty-seven years of marriage. My hat's off to them, and my heart will always hold them close. Enjoy their story!

Glenn and Lorine Allen

Glenn was the second of five children born to Eugene "Hoot" Allen and his wife Ethel Fitzgerald Allen. He was born on December 6, 1924. He said, "I was born in the cold and have been cold ever since!" When asked his middle name, Glenn offers, "Harris . . . and I don't have any idea where it came from." His siblings, in order of their birth, were: Dennis, Louise, Maxie, and Verna. Glenn said that Verna, as the youngest child, was spoiled, but everyone loved her. Of all the siblings, she died first at forty-four years of age. Of the five, Glenn and his brother Maxie still survive.

Glenn's maternal grandparents were Alfred and Lelia Fitzgerald, who owned a two-hundred acre farm on Fork Mountain. His paternal grandparents were Andy and Lucy Jane Allen, who lived on the North fork of the Tye River, just down

Glenn, Louise, and Maxie with their mother, Ethel

the mountain from where his parents' house was located up against Dowell's Ridge. Hoot bought fifty acres from his father and fifty acres from his older brother and built a house on the hundred-acre spread where Glenn and the other children were raised.

The Alfred Fitzgerald family; Glenn's mother, Ethel, is front row center

Glenn's parents, "Hoot" and Ethel Allen, at their Dowell's Ridge home

Hoot cut timber for a living, and the family had huge gardens in which grew vegetables that his mother canned in half-gallon jars. Back then, they canned outdoors in washtubs over an open fire. They had a root cellar and a basement, where potatoes and apples were kept over the winter. When autumn came, Hoot also bought a hundred pounds of dried pinto beans and fifty pounds of salt fish. Glenn remembers that the fish, which he thinks were herring, were his dad's favorite. They had to be soaked overnight to get the salt out before one could fry them.

The Allens also had an orchard of York apples, which they called "Johnsons," a few early yellow apples, and one Smokehouse tree. From these apples they made kettles of apple butter. Glenn never liked making the butter because of the amount of work involved. One had to peel from fifteen to twenty bushels of fruit the night before, then stir the kettle for most of the next day. He recalled, "My Uncle Les's wife had a fifty-gallon copper kettle, and she was very careful who she loaned it out to."

As a child, Glenn attended the Mill Creek School, which was located about a mile from his house just over Dowell's Ridge. It was a one-room schoolhouse, and one teacher taught all seven grades. He said that the Montebello School had an eighth grade. Glenn feels that kids back then got a better education because there weren't as many children in each class, and if they did have a problem, the teacher could give individual attention. He remembers one teacher who taught him to sound out his letters (phonics), and attributes that for his being able to read well throughout his life.

When he was in the sixth grade and Dennis was in the seventh, they decided to quit school and go to logging with their dad. "We was up on the hill by the barn in the big garden when we saw the teacher walking up to where we were. She said she was giving a test, and if we'd come back to school and take the test and pass it, she'd move us up to the next grade. We took the test and passed but never did go back to school!"

Glenn got additional education after he came home from the service and went to work at a company where he had to read blueprints and make drawings. He took an international correspondence course through the mail and studied business math, English, and algebra. Lorine studied the course along with her husband, and in later years, she attended Blue Ridge Community College to learn data processing and accounting. When their son Gary went to college, Lorine went to work at the Wayne-Tex plant in Waynesboro in the finance department; her last job there was making up payroll. She retired after twenty-three years of service.

After Glenn and Dennis quit school, both boys went to work logging with their dad. When Glenn was about fifteen years old, his dad put in a bid on a tract of land on which Mr. Dall Small had timber-selling rights; Hoot won the bid. The timber was part of the "Big Survey," where the present Wintergreen Ski Resort is now located in Nelson County. They cut what was called "extract wood," which was dead standing chestnut trees that blight had killed early in the 1900s. The old trees stood seventy-five to eighty foot tall and had hardly any limbs at the bottom.

The tract of land adjoined property that was owned by Hoot's sister, Bess, up on Fortune's Mountain. There was an abandoned house on the land, so the Allens brought their bedding and groceries on Sunday evenings, when they'd arrive at the site, and set up housekeeping during the week. They did all their own cooking. On Friday evenings, they would drive back home for the weekend.

Glenn said that the earliest truck he remembered his dad having was a 1927 Model T Ford that had a split windshield from which the top glass could be rolled out. They also had 1937 and 1940 Ford trucks that they used for hauling the logs to the mills. They would cut timber and take one load a day to a mill in either Lynchburg or Buena Vista. On Fridays, they would drive one last load to the mill and collect their check for the week. The three Allen men, and another man they'd hired to help log, worked four years on that one timber tract. In addition to the trucks, they had a horse to help pull the huge trees, that were cut with crosscut saws, out of the mountains.

Later they changed to a gasoline-powered, two-man chain saw that was a big step up from the early saws that required muscle and man power; they kept the old crosscuts, nevertheless. The men finally switched to individual chain saws when they became available, making the work of logging much easier.

One can never talk to any members of the extended Allen family without mentioning music, specifically bluegrass music. They are a mountain family that seems to be abundantly blessed with musical talent, both in the playing and singing. I remember Johnny Coffey telling me back in the 1980s that sisters Bessie and Estelle Allen played harmony fiddles so beautifully that it brought tears to his eyes. These two girls were Hoot's sisters.

Glenn was around six years old when he got his first mandolin. Everyone in Glenn's family played some type of stringed instrument, and he says it is much easier for a person to learn if family members know how. "It falls natural to someone when everybody else is playing."

His grandfather played the fiddle and sang. Hoot played the guitar and banjo and took fiddle lessons from a man by the name of Jim Chisolm, who taught music in Crozet. Glenn recalls that his dad played the guitar so much that he developed corns on his fingers. Dennis played guitar and later picked up the banjo. All they needed for bluegrass music was a mandolin and a high tenor. Glenn fit the bill, and at ten years old was playing and singing with his dad and brother Dennis on the WSVA radio station in Harrisonburg, where they broadcast from the fourth floor of the courthouse.

At the same time, Hoot's brother Pug Allen and Pug's two daughters were playing at the same radio station. Bill Monroe is thought to have been the one bluegrass music was named for. Until that time, the same type of music was simply known as "old-time." Monroe was from Kentucky, and the style in which he played was dubbed bluegrass, after the blue-green color of the grass grown in that state. When Pug's son, George, picked up the fiddle, Hoot switched to the banjo; around the 1950s, the four Allens plus Neil Mace formed a bluegrass group called "The Skyline Boys," who were very popular throughout the years.

Dennis, Glenn, and Hoot Allen

In 2001, a group called "The New Skyline Boys" got together when Glenn's great nephew, Jerry Allen, decided he wanted to play. Four members of the Allen family (Glenn and George from the original group, Bucky and Jerry, their great-nephews) and Ricky Strickler still play on occasion. Glenn's son Gary also filled in for Jerry when he couldn't make a gig.

Going back to the early years, Glenn said that he had always known Lorine because their parents had known one another since

The Skyline Boys: Neil Mace and Pug, Glenn, Hoot, and George Allen

The New Skyline Boys

they were young. They didn't see each other all the time because their families lived in two different communities, but the Allens would often drive by the Coffeys' house. Lorine remembers that Glenn, who was around twelve years old at the time, would come to White Rock Church, where she attended, and sit behind her. She thought he was awfully nice and sang the old hymns so beautifully. She also knew that he sang on the radio, which made him seem pretty exciting to a young girl.

Glenn recalls that he saw Lorine one day when they were teenagers and thought, "I'd like to keep her." Lorine remembers that her house was always filled with young people, and Glenn came to make music with her cousin, Elwood Taylor. It wasn't long before the two were dating.

Glenn's naval photo

At age nineteen, Glenn enlisted in the Navy; when he left for boot camp in Norfolk, he and Lorine were already engaged. He had been deferred for a year because the military considered logging to be defense work. The extract wood was made into tannic acid, which was used to cure shoes, saddles, and other leather goods. But Glenn had had enough of deferment, so he went on to enlist. He came home for one week after boot camp and was then sent with a whole trainload of recruits to Newport, Rhode Island, where they trained before being shipped out to the Pacific on the USS *Pittsburg* on January 13, 1945.

Glenn's ship, the *USS Pittsburg*

Glenn explained that each man trained for a specific job on the ship and did it to the best of his ability, knowing that everyone's lives depended on it. Glenn's official title was seaman first class, and he was a trainer on five-inch gun mounts from May 15, 1944, through February 4, 1946. Glenn was responsible for the horizontal positioning on the heavy cruiser of the huge gun mounts that shot down planes trying to bomb the ship. He had a friend whose job was to point the guns vertically, and it took thirteen men to operate each individual gun mount.

Glenn was part of two of the biggest invasions during the war: Iwo Jima and Okinawa, Iwo Jima being the worst of the two. On March 19, 1945, the *USS Franklin* was bombed by a single Japanese plane, devastating its decks, igniting fires, and knocking out communication. Fifty miles off the Japanese mainland, the *Frank-*

Gun mounts on the USS Pittsburg

The USS Franklin after it had been bombed

lin lay dead in the water. The *Pittsburg* was called in to tow the injured carrier. The *Franklin* was towed away from danger and was later able to proceed safely under its own power to Pearl Harbor for repairs.

Glenn remembers that the enemy planes tried to disable both ships, but the *Pittsburg* was able to provide the needed defense, and the *Franklin* was brought to safety. Casualties totaled 724 seamen killed and 265 wounded, making the *Franklin* the most heavily damaged aircraft carrier during the war.

On June 5, the *USS Pittsburg* was also involved in one of the biggest naval errors made during that time. An admiral sent the entire task group on a route that led it straight into a typhoon that had seventy-knot winds and one hundred-foot waves. The carrier was dashed in the waves and lost 104 feet of its bow. Miraculously, not a man was lost, thanks to the crew's masterful seamanship. The wounded ship battled the typhoon for seven hours before the storm subsided, and on June 10, it docked at Guam for repairs. The ship made it back to dry dock and was then sent back to the States for a new bow; it was at Puget Sound Naval Shipyard when the war ended.

When the war was over, Glenn was discharged. He rode the train for four days and four nights back to Waynesboro. When he returned, he lived at his parents' home and worked with his dad for a few months before marrying Lorine. About his time in the military, Glenn continues to say that the Navy was very good to him, and it was an honor to serve his country.

All this time, Lorine was waiting in the Virginia mountains for her fiancé to return, never knowing if he'd make it back or not. Luckily, things worked out for the best, and Glenn and Lorine were married on November 2, 1946, by Rev. Charles Krause at the parsonage of Vesuvius Baptist Church.

At that time, Hoot and Dennis were operating a Frick sawmill they had purchased from Lorine's father, Hercy Coffey. Dennis sold his part to Glenn, so Hoot and Glenn ran it together for a time. It was at this point in the interview that Lorine offered, "Yes, he got my dad's saw and his daughter." Not to be outdone,

Glenn shot back, "And he was glad to get rid of both of them!" When we all quit laughing, Glenn said that he continued to run the mill until his father became disabled, and Glenn didn't want to work without him.

The couple's first home was an apartment in a large house in Steeles Tavern, where Lorine's sister and her husband, their aunt, and cousins were living. While there, their first son, Gary, was born at the Lexington Hospital on October 30, 1947.

The Allens next moved to a tenant house on Lofton Road and lived there for about a year and a half before buying a 113-acre farm with a house in Greenville; they lived there long enough for Glenn to know he didn't want to be a farmer! He remembers paying $2,800 for the whole place.

The final move came in 1951, when they bought their present home at White Hill in Stuarts Draft, a stone cottage that they made improvements to as they went along. It didn't have indoor plumbing or water inside to start with, but they corrected that situation and later added several more rooms. Gary was three years old and recalls lying in the back seat of the car while they were moving and seeing the moon as they rounded the last curve toward home.

Four years later, on July 17, 1954, their younger son, Steve, was born at King's Daughters' Hospital in Staunton. The boys were raised at White Hill and called it home. Lorine said they liked the community they'd moved into and soon became part of the neighborhood activities.

The boys had friends in the neighborhood, at their church, and at school. Gary married Denise and has a daughter, Whitney, who in January 2013 made Glenn and Lorine great-grandparents for the fourth time. They currently live in Ivy. Steve is married to Shanna; he has two daughters, Carrie and Kaitlyn, who have two boys and a girl between them (Rowan, Aiden, and Ryleigh). Steve and Shanna live right down the road from his parents in Stuarts Draft.

Glenn found employment after marriage at Virginia Metalcrafters in Waynesboro. The company was first located along the South River where it manufactured Loth stoves. The owner wanted to make a change to the gift business, and the brass foundry was the main part of that department. Glenn said that it was very difficult to melt down the brass. He worked in the foundry for a time but began having trouble with his lungs, and the doctor recommended he be transferred to another section.

He took over the stove and lawn mower division, where hundreds of Penn 88 riding lawn mowers were made. An engineer by the name of Dr. Gordon had the original mower; after his death, Glenn bought the mower from his wife and took it home. Glenn's son Steve completely restored it. Glenn is pictured with the finished lawn mower that he still has today. Glenn worked for the company for thirty-nine years and retired in 1985.

By the time he and Lorine moved to their Stuarts Draft home, Glenn had all but quit singing and playing bluegrass music. It just got to be too much running around, and he wanted to spend more time with his family. Also, an accident at work had left Glenn without his right index finger, which he needed to play the mandolin. It wasn't until

Glenn alongside his Penn 88 mower

1971 when Gary wanted his dad to teach him guitar that Glenn picked up his instruments and once again began to play.

The Allens were attending White Hill Church of the Brethren, and a gospel quartet was formed with Mervin and Ruby Miller, Margie Campbell, and Glenn. They called themselves the Brethrenaires and were always in demand for performances at area churches. Lorine said of all the music her husband ever did, this

Glenn playing his mandolin (1976)

was her favorite. In 1986, the unthinkable happened. Glenn contracted cancer of the larynx and went through laser surgery and twenty-five days of radiation. For three months afterward, he did not talk, much less sing. The doctors told him that he would probably never sing again, but Glenn, always the trooper, began to sing a little after three months of silence. "I never could sing as long as I used to," said Glenn, but he's been at it ever since and has had no reoccurrence of the cancer.

Before Lorine's father passed away, her mother, Burgess, promised him that she wouldn't live by herself if anything happened to him. So after his death in 1956, she began living with her three daughters, alternating between them. In 1959, Lorine began to have thyroid problems and became so weak she could hardly get around. Burgess came to stay with the family to help out in any way she could. Glenn was working and had two young sons plus a large garden to take care of. Gary, who was twelve at the time, recalls with a great deal of fondness how he learned how to cook, wash dishes, and clean house under his grandmother's tutelage.

"She was here all the time but never intrusive. She'd get Steve and me up for school, fix us breakfast, making anything we wanted, including tomato gravy and 'egg-in-a-hole.' It was an amazing thing and was a great experience until our mother could get better."

Burgess stayed on for about ten years, and when her daughter Lura's husband died, she moved to Spottswood to help her, too. Burgess was one of the most giving and kind women I have ever met. In fact, Glenn gave his mother-in-law one of the finest com-

Burgess Coffey, Glenn's mother-in-law

pliments I've ever heard come from a man: "She was the best person I've ever known in my lifetime. It's an absolute fact . . . nobody was ever any better."

Late in life, Burgess took up oil painting, and the family has many of her beautiful art pieces gracing their homes. In 1993, Lorine herself began taking art lessons from Sylvia Morris, a very talented artist from Nellysford. Along with her mother's work, Lorine's home is filled with her own lovely acrylic paintings of places and things that are meaningful to the family.

Glenn has a love of fishing that he's carried throughout his life, and everyone wanted me to hear Glenn's "fish story." Seems that his niece Ann saw a huge trout in a deep hole behind her

Glenn fishing in the Tye River

cabin along the Tye River. She wouldn't let anyone fish for it until her Uncle Glenn came and tried his luck. He put a salmon egg on a hook, and soon there were people lining the bank watching Glenn trying to catch that fish. He finally pulled in the whopper, which was indeed huge!

I can remember that the night before trout season opened, the same tiny mountain community of White Rock was a bustle of activity with people visiting and playing bluegrass music at all the camps along the river. It is a memory I will always treasure and one that everyone misses.

I asked how life was different now from when they were growing up. Glenn said, "Back then you had jobs to do, and all of it was physical. We plowed our land with horses and hoed our corn by hand. We always had plenty to eat, but we had to work hard in order to get it. Lorine's parents ran a sawmill, a gristmill, as well as a little store where people could buy things. Teachers spent more time with the children and made frequent visits to the homes, often spending the night. Weather didn't stop us from going to school. We'd stomp our way through snow that had a layer of ice on top. Winters were much worse back then, and once the snow started to fall, it stayed on the ground until spring."

Glenn and Lorine at Glens Falls in Vesuvius, Virginia

A "cousins' day" held at the White Rock homeplace (2010)

Lorine said that their work ethic was such that "We worked hard to have a good life in the mountains, and once we moved here to Stuarts Draft, we worked hard to keep having a good life. I never take for granted what we have. When I turn on the faucet and hot water comes out or when we turn up the heat in the furnace to get warm, it is such a good feeling to have more comforts than we did back in the mountains."

The interview came to a close, but we continued to sit around the kitchen table talking, drinking coffee, and eating the pecan pie

Glenn holding his great-granddaughter, Ryleigh

Lorine had fixed us. Glenn said that he wanted one more thing included in the new book. "We've had a good life. The Lord has really been good to us. I don't know why because we surely don't deserve it, but he has always been a big part of our life."

As I prepared to leave, I hugged Glenn. When he said, "We love you," a sudden wave of emotion hit me. These people . . . these mountain people whom folks said would never accept outsiders, have not only accepted me but gathered me up under their wings like a mother hen gathers her chicks. They've included me in their reunions, picnics, and "cousins' day" get-togethers; sharing their lives, their families, and their hearts with the little Florida flat-lander who, by God's grace, found her forever place among them in the Blue Ridge Mountains of Virginia.

Ora Coffey Smith (Stuarts Draft)

Madeline Grant at her Montebello home

8

Madeline White Grant

At ninety-one years of age, Madeline is one hard lady to keep up with. She is always on the go and finds the inconvenience of a hip replacement just that—inconvenient. Last year she had her second her hip surgery because the woman keeps wearing them out!

I met Madeline, her husband, Wilson, and her sweet family of children long before I ever moved here. The Grants have run the Montebello Country Store, campground, and trout fishing pond for many years. When my family would visit the area back in the 1970s, invariably we would stop at the store for a soft drink and some conversation. But it wasn't until I moved here permanently and began publishing the *Backroads* newspaper that I got to know the Grants on a more personal level.

The older I get, the more I find that life holds many surprises, so it wasn't until I interviewed Madeline for *Appalachian Heart* that I was made aware of the hardships of her early childhood. There's an old saying about the trials of living: they can either make you bitter or better. You would never know from talking with Madeline that she's endured some rough patches in her life. She is one of the most upbeat, positive people I've ever met, full of good humor and encouragement for others. She has chosen to be in the "better" camp, and I was honored when she said she'd let met interview her for the book. Madeline Grant has one of the biggest Appalachian hearts of anybody I know, and I am pleased to write her life story. Enjoy!

Mary Madeline White was born on February 19, 1922, to parents Albert White and Bessie Weaver White, who were living at that time in Covington, Virginia. Bessie's people were from Covington, and Albert was originally from North Dakota. Madeline was the second child of five, but the three born after her died. Madeline's older sister, Louise Virginia, was born on August 15, 1920. Pearl Edden was born and died on March 25, 1923. An unnamed girl was born and died on December 19, 1924, and a boy, Albert J. E. White, was born on March 7, 1925, but died four months later on July 11.

Madeline's father, Albert White

Bessie, who had been born on October 17, 1900, died of milk fever at twenty-five years of age while the family was living in Canonsburg, Pennsylvania, where Madeline's father was employed on the railroad. Madeline was two and a half years old at the time, and Louise was almost five. Bessie had long dark hair, and when she died and was laid out on a cot in the living room, Madeline remembers rubbing her hair. Madeline was given an old family Bible by her grandfather that stated that he had paid for perpetual care for his daughter's grave for as long as the cemetery was active.

Because there was no one in Pennsylvania to care for the girls while Albert worked, he moved them back to Covington, closer to his wife's family. Bessie had several sisters living there, and

Madeline said that she and Louise stayed with them for several months, but somehow it never worked out for them to stay on permanently. With a child's reasoning, Madeline said that she felt it was because she was such a tomboy at that young age, and her aunts didn't like the way she was always climbing trees and playing outside. As an adult, she knows that wasn't the case but never did pursue finding out why the aunts had not wanted to keep the girls.

Madeline's mother, Bessie, holding either Madeline or Louise

After that, they went to live with their dad for a time, but he had a job and a lot of personal problems that made it impossible for him to properly care for his daughters, so they spent a lot of time with neighbors who took pity on the two motherless children. They lived this way for a few years, but Madeline said that when she was around five years old, Social Services was notified. The girls became wards of the state, were separated, and were put into foster homes in the Covington area. It wasn't until many years later that the sisters found each other and were reunited. As a child, Madeline reasoned, "I didn't know for a long time where my sister was, and I thought if I only had a brother, he would take care of me."

Madeline lived in five different homes through the years. I asked how she felt inside as a child. She said that she always had the feeling that things weren't right. That she wasn't welcome. "All I knew was to move somewhere . . . to be ready to go somewhere else." One of the first families she lived with was a man and wife who worked at the silk mill in Covington. They had property on Irish Creek and took Madeline with them to live in a small home there.

Across the road lived the Ernest Grant family; they had two girls about the same age as Madeline and a son by the name of Wilson, who was a few years older than Madeline. More often than not, she was over at their house playing with them. It got so that she didn't want to go back home, and the Grant girls, Dolly and Agnes, would hide Madeline in the attic when her foster parents came looking for her.

The Grant home where Madeline played (and later lived) in her early years

Madeline remembers living with a Parks family in Big Island; then she was placed in a home in Waynesboro but spent only one night there before realizing that the people only wanted a servant to clean the house and wait on them. The next morning, after they left for work, she packed her bag and walked to the home of Dolly Layton, whose house was just down the street. Dolly was the older sister of Wilson Grant, and she welcomed the child and let her live there with her until Social Services got involved again.

This time, Madeline went back to Irish Creek to live with the Grant family, whom Madeline said were very good to her. She lived there for a time before finally settling in with Wilson's grandparents, Dick and Dolly Seaman, who lived in the heart of Montebello. Madeline was around sixteen years old by then, and she got along fine with the Seaman family.

The extended Grant family included her in all their activities, and she said, "The Grants had a truck, and they would take me places. We'd all pile in the back of the truck and go to a fair, the movies, or just to town to shop.

Madeline as a teenager at Ernest Grant's house

"One time, Grandma [Dolly] Seaman got mad at me for something—I can't remember what—and said she was writing a letter to Social Services to come get me. She put the letter in the mail and told me to pack my bags and get ready to move, because they'd be coming to take me back. I did as I was told, but a few days went by, then a week, and no one showed up. Grandpa Seaman, when he had something important to say, would clear his throat. One day, he cleared his throat and called me over to him. He said, 'I'm going to tell you something, but I don't want you to tell Dolly. I went and got that

Dick and Dolly Seaman

letter out of the mailbox, so they aren't coming after you. I knew she'd cool off after a little while.'" Madeline laughed and said, "Nothing more was ever said about it."

Around this time, she received a letter from her sister, Louise, who was married and living in New Jersey with a family of her own. Louise had changed her name to "Helena," and when I asked Madeline why she changed her name, she couldn't give me a direct answer but said, "Maybe to forget everything that happened to her and have a fresh start. I found out later that she did not fare as well as I did in the foster homes where she was placed. I was treated good in every home I lived." Madeline heard later that her father had been killed crossing a four-lane road when he was about fifty years old and was taken back to Ohio for burial.

Once Madeline moved in with the Seaman's, she walked to the Montebello School to attend classes and to Mount Paran Baptist Church for Sunday services. She recalls with a laugh how she would wear old shoes to walk to church, carrying her good shoes, which she then changed into out by the fence. She'd hide her old shoes in the bushes, then change back into them for the walk home.

Pupils at the Montebello School in earlier times

She remembers that Montebello had several stores. One of them, Barnett's and Robertson's, also housed the post office. There was also a store and post office located at Wilkie, a little farther up the road. There was a mill just up Fork Mountain Road, where people came to have their grain ground, and Madeline now has both mill stones on her property: one in the yard, the other inside the Montebello Store. When Madeline was living with the Seaman family, the Montebello Store closed. It was later reopened when Hansford and Flora Grant bought the property and began their business there.

The Montebello Store in the early years

It was at about this time that Madeline's sister wrote and sent her money for a bus ticket to New Jersey, telling her to come live with her. That morning before church that Sunday, Madeline packed her bag and had every intention of hitching a ride to the bus station after services. Wilson Grant found out about her plans and told her that if she left, they might never see each other again. Madeline said that she thought about what he'd said and decided right then to stay in Montebello.

Wilson was still in high school and drove the bus from Irish Creek to the school in Fairfield. At the time, Madeline was dating a few local boys; one in particular was kind of sweet on her, but she didn't return his feelings. He would show up at the Seaman residence and play the guitar for her, but she found herself hiding from him. One day he showed up at the door, and Dick Seaman called up the stairs to Madeline, "If you don't want to see him, you need to tell him so." Madeline did tell him and said after that he never came back.

When she was nineteen, Madeline began dating Wilson exclusively, and they courted for several years before marrying on March 26, 1943; she was twenty-one and Wilson was twenty-four. By this time, Wilson had left Montebello and had gotten a job as a steamfitter at the shipyard in Newport News. Madeline found work on base as well, at the Newport News shipyard commissary, and was living at a boarding house run by the Phelps family. The

Wilson and Madeline on their wedding day

couple went to a justice of the peace to get married. Madeline remembers wearing a navy blue suit, white blouse, fancy hat, and white gloves. Mrs. Phelps and her daughter stood up for them at the ceremony.

The couple moved in with Wilson's parents down on Irish Creek for a time and later moved in with his grandparents, Dolly and Dick Seaman, where Madeline had lived as a teenager years before. Wilson cut timber, raised crops, and did work on the farm.

The Grants were still living on Irish Creek when their first son, Roosevelt Wilson, Jr. ("R. W."), was born on January 14, 1944. These were the war years; Wilson enlisted in the Marine Corps in June 1944 and was stationed at Camp Lejeune, North Carolina. Madeline had a car and drove down to spend time with him whenever she could. She stayed in a little cabin off base.

One night about ten o'clock in the evening, Wilson slipped away from the barracks to tell her to leave immediately, that he was being shipped out the next morning. She drove home and didn't hear from him for about two or three months. Wilson served for over a year in California, Guam, and Okinawa. He came home in May 1946.

When he returned, they continued to live at the Grant homeplace, and Madeline remembers painting the house and the trees with whitewash so that everything outside would look nice. Their second child, Patricia Marie, was born on March 27, 1947, and both she and R. W. were delivered by Wilson's mother, Flora, who was a certified midwife. The

The Grant family: (left to right)
Charles, R. W., Patricia, Wilson, and Madeline

youngest child, Charles Downey, was born on April 6, 1949, at the hospital in Lexington, Virginia.

The family's next move was to New Ellington, South Carolina, where the DuPont plant, based in Waynesboro, was managing the Savannah River Project, which was going to be a hydrogen bomb manufacturing plant. The family stayed in South Carolina for three years until the project was completed before moving back to Montebello. By then, Wilson's grandfather, Dick Seaman, had died, so the Grants moved in with his grandmother, Dolly.

Around 1953, Wilson found employment on the Blue Ridge Parkway as a laborer in the maintenance department. Some of his early co-workers on the Parkway were Gordon Demastus, Jake Hewitt, Saylor Coffey, Troy Painter, Earl Ramsey, Milton and Gorman Bryant, Delbert Seaman, Mitchael Seaman, Attibell Farris, and Danny Myrtle. The men cut trees, opened the overlooks, mowed grass, poured curbing, patched the road, and did anything else that needed to be done.

Madeline said Wilson worked with some great people who put her husband in a position for advancement. In January 1960, the family made another move to Big Island, Virginia, where Wilson was promoted to district supervisor for the maintenance department for the James River district. They stayed in Big Island until summer 1962, when Wilson and the family moved once again; this time to Spruce Pine, North Carolina. In 1963, it was back to Big Island, where they made Wilson maintenance supervisor from Rockfish Gap to Vinton, Virginia.

Madeline laughed as she told me that they'd lived in one of the two ranger houses on the Parkway; the other one was occupied by the chief ranger, Dan Lee. "So we had Lee and Grant living right next to each other." In 1971 they were moved down to Asheville, North Carolina and stayed until Wilson retired in June of 1975 after he began to have problems with arthritis. It was at this time the Grants moved back to Montebello permanently.

Hansford and Flora Grant's fiftieth wedding anniversary

Wilson's mother, Flora Grant, ran the Montebello Store until she passed away in 1968. The store remained closed until two of Madeline's grown children (Patty and Charles) moved back to

Montebello and opened it back up in 1972. At the same time, Walter Hoffman was contracted to dig a fishing pond across from the store where people could come to fish for trout. This was a big attraction. Madeline said that on the opening day of season, the pond—which was stocked with about two thousand rainbow trout—would be completely fished out, and several tons of fish would have to be ordered for the following day.

"Dutch" Cash at the Montebello Store

A campground was added adjacent to the store and pond, and it became a destination for people wanting to escape city life to enjoy the mountain solitude Montebello offered. After Wilson's retirement, the Grants became the main storekeepers and managers of the resort's pond and campground.

For a short time, the couple lived in Wilson's mother's home next to the store, but later they moved into the four-room house they owned at the rear of the store and added more rooms over the years. Madeline said that when they first moved back to Montebello, Milton and Doris Bryant were living in the little house, but then they bought land from Hazel Seaman on Fork Mountain and built their own place.

At this time, the Montebello post office was located in Homer Anderson's store, but when he closed his doors (around 1980), the Grants began housing the post office in one corner of their store. Because Wilson was on disability, Madeline was recruited to be the new postmaster. At first she didn't think she could do the job, but Wilson encouraged her, and she began to think, "I can sell stamps, sort the mail, and keep records, and, really, that is the bottom line." After Madeline sorted the day's mail, people could come into the store to pick it up.

Joe Seaman later became the postmaster at the store, and Madeline served as his assistant. In 1985, the postal service decided to construct a separate building for the Montebello post office, and the Grants leased them the land and paid for construction of the new facility. Joe continued on as postmaster when the office moved from the store to the new building. The rural route carrier at that time was Junior Hatter, who delivered out Fork Mountain and down the North Fork to Tyro.

Around 1982, the Grants, as well as many community members, thought that the village should have a fire department of its own, since the closest one was in Raphine at the time. Wilson and Madeline donated the land on which a permanent building could be built, and the Floyd Groah family did the actual construction. Around 1984, a rescue squad was added, and both still serve the community today.

The business has always had family members working in it. For some of the time, Patty and her husband, Felton Hendrix, managed the store and campground with her parents, then in 1992, the Grant's youngest son, Charles, and his wife, Vicki, bought

The Montebello Store (2013)

Wilson and Madeline's fiftieth anniversary

the Montebello Camping/Fishing Resort and have made many improvements over the years. The store has grown from a two-room building into a spacious structure filled with quality gifts and souvenirs, and there is a large new wing, complete with a huge fireplace, that serves breakfast and lunch on the weekends, May through December. It continues to be a place that locals and visitors to the area love to come because they always receive a warm welcome.

On November 23, 1998, Wilson passed away after fifty-six years of marriage; his plucky wife, Madeline, has continued to be a vital part of the Montebello community and is still a familiar face at the store. She is a very busy lady, and one would never guess that she will celebrate her ninety-first birthday in 2013. She even tenderly watches over the Cash sisters, Frances and Mary, driving them to town to do their shopping whenever they want to go and making sure they have what they need.

In addition to her three children, Madeline now has twelve grandchildren, eighteen great-grandchildren, and five great-great-grandchildren, with another on the way at this writing. She is kind and generous and filled with good humor that makes

Madeline relaxing at home

her endearing to all who know her. Though an "orphan" with a rough start, Madeline's outlook has always been positive, and she is quick to say, "I've had a good life. You can't carry bad things around with you; you need to get rid of them and go on with your life. My mother would have been like that. I trust in the Lord, and he's taken care of me my whole life. Even as a child, I knew he was watching over and taking care of me."

Madeline's final words reminded me of my own favorite verse in the Bible, Jeremiah 29:11, that says, "I know the plans I have for you, saith the Lord. They are plans for good and not for evil, to give you a future and a hope."

Robert Rexrode (Kerr's Creek)

Clemon Lee Lawhorne

9

Clemon Lee Lawhorne

As with so many of the other mountain people, I'm not exactly sure where I first met Clemon and his wife, Peggy. I probably met Peggy first, when she worked at Flippin-Seaman Orchard in Tyro and I stopped in to buy a bushel of fall apples. But they were also at many of the reunions and church homecomings that I've gone to over the years. They've invited me and Billy to their summer pig roast held the last Saturday in August, and we've bumped into them at bluegrass sings in people's garages. Wherever and whenever we see them, it's always a pleasure to talk and catch up on what's happening on their side of the ridge.

We live in the hamlet of Love at the top of Campbell's Mountain Road; the Lawhornes live at the bottom of Campbell's Mountain Road on Cox's Creek in Tyro. Our houses are only six miles apart but to get to either one, we have to drive a steep, narrow gravel road across a good-sized mountain that separates us.

I planned on interviewing Clemon on December 18, 2012, and for the whole month, the weather had been unusually warm. This particular day, however, was much cooler, and the wind had a bite to it. At one point, while we were sitting around the kitchen table, Peggy pointed out the window and said, "Look!" A snow shower was blowing through, but a few minutes later, it stopped as abruptly as it had started.

Peggy sliced off a piece of apple cake and gave it to me, and I commented on how good it was. She laughed and said, "Lila Lee came to visit me yesterday." Lila Campbell is one of the Lawhornes' neighbors, and I had stopped at her house before coming to the Lawhornes'. As I was walking out her door, she handed me one of those cakes, still hot from the oven! That's one of the nicest things I've learned about the mountain people—you always leave with more than you brought.

Today Lila gave me an apple cake, and when I left Clem and Peggy's, my arms were filled with a bag of Fuji apples (she still works at the orchard) and an 1835 map of the area that Clem had reproduced. To say nothing of the envelope full of vintage photographs they lent me to make copies of for *Appalachian Heart* and their stories of growing up along Cox's Creek. I hope I can do justice in writing Clem's precious memories of a time that only a few can still remember.

Both Clem and Peggy are very humble people, content to stay in the background with no thought of tooting their own horn, but the longer I know them, the more I realize these are the folks that have the most to offer. Clem said he quit school in his teens to help out on the family farm, but the lack of a higher education

Looking down Cox's Creek; the tree in the center was an American chestnut

has never stopped the inquisitiveness he possessed as a child or the pursuit of finding out how things operate. His mind is always working, and he can just look at a problem and figure out what's needed to fix it. He's quick, inventive, and pretty humorous to boot! His mind holds the secrets and the history of the place where he was born, raised, and continues to live—Cox's Creek.

Clem relates that the first record of any Lawhorne in this particular part of Nelson County was his great-grandfather on his father's side, Daniel Lawhorne, who came from the Indian Creek area of Amherst County, Virginia. Daniel's son, Zachariah, was Clem's grandfather. Zach was born in a log cabin just up Cox's Creek from where Clem now lives.

A story was always told that there was a large persimmon tree behind Zach's house that had a grape vine growing in it. Clem's father, Lee, used to tell his children not to bother the vine because his grandfather had brought it from Amherst County when he moved here in 1850. The vine was there when Daniel applied for a marriage license in 1855 to wed his wife Bessie. In turn, Zach married Ella Campbell, a close relative of Jonah Campbell who lived up on Shoe Creek.

When Zach married Ella, they built a new cabin below his father's home, closer to the creek at the mouth of the hollow;

Upstream on Cox's Creek, looking down on Clem's house at the bottom

Zach's wife, Ella Campbell Lawhorne (Clem's grandmother)

that's where Clem's father, Lee, was born. At that time, the land was cleared and had crops growing all the way to the top, so when around 1900 there was a flood, the ground washed away and the family woke to find mud and rocks running through the windows. Zach then took the cabin down and moved it back against the foot of the mountain, out of the mouth of the hollow and away from the spring branch that had flooded.

I asked Clem if this little hollow had always been called Cox's Creek. He said yes, as far back as he could find any old records. He said that a Cox family had lived high on the mountain at the head of the creek at a place the bear hunters call the "potato patch," and the creek is thought

Zachariah and Ella's cabin on Cox's Creek (early 1900s)

to be named after the people who lived there.

He explained that in the 1830s, the Massie family had built a carriage road from Massies Mill to Steeles Tavern that followed the Tye River all the way up the mountain. The road originated at Level Green Plantation, wound around to Pharsalia Plantation, and came up between the Big DePriest and Little DePriest mountains around the head of Cox's Creek. The Crabtree road was

Zachariah Lawhorne with one of his granddaughters

part of the main road that went to Montebello and beyond. This former road, known as the Tye River Turnpike, is now part of the present Route 56. The map that Clem gave me is an actual 1935 survey that has all the bearings and boundary lines marked along the early road, as well as land owners, creeks, spring branches, mills, and iron-ore furnaces.

Clem's grandparents on his mother's side were William Lawhorne and Lillie Lawhorne Lawhorne; Clem's father, Lee, married their daughter, Julia. From Daniel's arrival in 1850, most of the Lawhorne family members continued to live up and down Cox's Creek.

Clem grew up at the homeplace at the top of the creek, and some of the neighbors besides all the Lawhornes who lived there

*Clem's great-grandmother, Avarilla Lawhorne
(wife of James Lewis Lawhorne)*

were members of the Campbell and Fitzgerald families. The Dunning family owned property also, and Clem said that the house and sixty-four acres where he and Peggy presently live was the old Dunning place.

Clem and all his siblings were born at the upper homeplace and were delivered by Leasy Snead Adams, a midwife who lived on Harper's Creek. The Lawhorne children, in order of their births, were: Elmer in 1937; Sam in 1938; Clemon on August 22, 1939; Ray in 1941; Donald in 1943; Betty in 1945; and one

Rufus Lawhorne with his work donkey

child after Betty, who died at birth. Of the six children, three survive: Clem, Ray, and Betty.

I asked what life was like when Clem was young, and he replied, "We grew up working. We carried water from the time we were six years old from the spring down under the hill. We carried water to wash clothes, to cook with, or for drinking water. There was no

Lee Roy Lawhorne with his ox, Old Red

Rare photo of Elwood Dunning, who married Lee Lawhorne's sister, Mattie

one living above us, so the creek was just as clean as the spring, and we used to carry water from both. In the wintertime, Mama would heat the water on her cookstove and pour it in a washtub and scrub clothes with a washboard in the house. If the weather was bad, she'd hang the clothes inside the house, but if the sun was shining, she'd hang them on a line in the yard. We had colder winters back then and a lot more snow."

Clem said that as far back as he can remember, they always had a garden. When his grandmother Ella was still living, she worked in the garden from daylight till dark, tending the plants. She would go

The old Dunning home on Cox's Creek (it later burned down)

up to the barn and get dried manure. She'd put it in a washtub and place the tub on some brush to drag it to the garden to fertilize the vegetables. Clem said that she was very particular and would only allow his oldest brother to work in the garden. If one of the

Clem's parents, Lee and Julia Lawhorne

Julia Ann Lawhorne and her six children

Clem's homeplace at the top of Cox's Creek

younger children wanted her for something, they had to stand at the gate and wait until she came out.

"You didn't set your foot inside her garden, because she didn't want us stepping on something." Clem laughed as he said, "I could resent that until this day . . . the garden was her sacred ground. She could grow the biggest watermelons I ever saw. I was about five years old, but I can remember how some of the bigger boys from the neighborhood would slip in there and sneak a big old watermelon. If she would have caught them, she would a put a stick on 'em, now!

"She could raise anything: watermelons, cantaloupes, sweet potatoes, Irish potatoes, beans, and she had these Spicewood bushes that she used for pickling. She planted them up against a big rock so Daddy couldn't plow them up with the turn plow. She also had a big patch of seven-year onions at the end of the garden that always stayed in the ground, and Daddy had to work the horse around them when he plowed in the spring.

"As soon as Grandma died and Daddy started working the garden, the first thing he did was plow under her onion patch and pull up those Spicewood bushes. In later years, we quit making the garden there at the house because the soil was so sandy with a lot of gravel in it. The reason, I think, is that this hollow here must have been an ancient landslide. You can dig down in that garden and you don't need sand or gravel to mix cement. I've taken shovelfuls of that soil and put it in a cement mixer with cement and poured footings on buildings that are still standing."

Growing up alongside a bold creek, I asked Clem if they were allowed to play in it. A big smile spread across his face as he told me, "Mama would have to run us out because the first warm day come, us boys would be in the creek until our lips would be turned blue. We'd be in that cold water right up till the first frost in the fall. There was a waterfall that had cut out a hole about four feet deep, and we dammed up the lower end to have us a good swimming hole with a rock to jump off of. That's where all of us kids learned to swim when we were five or six years old."

I asked about funerals in the early days, and Clem said that the first one he remembers was for his Aunt Kate, who died young. They buried her in the Lawhorne cemetery up on Cox's Creek; it was in the winter, and the men had to clear away a bunch of wild honeysuckle from the place she was to be buried. Relatives and friends helped dig the grave by hand. That was a common practice, and Clem said that he has helped dig graves from the top of Jack's Hill down to Jonesboro Baptist Church.

Clem handed me a photo of a man in front of an old car and explained that it was Roscoe Floyd, who carried the mail from Roseland to Montebello in the1940s up until Junior Hatter took over the route. He had an old Model A Ford, and when it snowed about six inches, the car made three sets of tracks: two tracks from the tires and the third from the transmission that would drag in the snow.

Clemon started school in the little one-room building located next to the Harmony Presbyterian Church at the end of Cox's Creek. It was known simply as the Harmony School, and Clem finished the fourth grade there before it closed down. The children were sent to Fleetwood School, where he finished the fifth, sixth, and seventh grades. Miss Lillian Jane Sanford was his teacher at both schools.

Roscoe Floyd, mail carrier from the late 1930s to the mid-1950s on the Montebello to Roseland route

Clem went to school until he was sixteen years old; that year, his daddy kept him out for about four weeks to get the corn crop in, and at the end of that time, Clem decided he wouldn't go back. He said that back then, none of his family had gone to school, and his father could print his name but could not write it in cursive. But Lee could figure numbers faster in his head than someone could do it with a pencil and paper. Lee was a farmer

Harmony School and the church

Harmony Presbyterian Church members at Cox's Creek (1920)

most of his life and later worked for the highway department in the early 1940s when they were constructing Route 56. Around 1946, they began construction of the Back Creek Road from Sherando up to Love, and Clemon's dad told him they dug the bridges by hand.

Clem stayed at home and cropped the land until he was nineteen years old; then he got a job at Morton Frozen Foods in Crozet. He needed a car for transportation to and from work and bought a 1955 Chevy sport coupe, two-door hardtop, for which he paid $1,550.00. He stated that it was a real classic, one of only fourteen hundred made, and he kicks himself for trading it later for a 1963 Chevy II. The salesman's son was standing by with a set of tags; when the deal was made, the boy put them on the '55. Clem heard that the boy had rolled the car that following weekend. Clem said thinking about it still makes him sick.

I asked if he had dated anyone up to this time, and Clem said no, he stayed mostly to himself. But there was a girl by the name of Peggy Lawhorne (daughter of John Leslie Lawhorne and Lena Bell Jones Lawhorne) who lived up the road in the house where Lila Lee Campbell now lives. When she was nine, her family moved up on Cox's Creek, so she and Clem grew up together in the same place.

Clem said that before he bought his first car, practically every night he and a bunch of other boys went hunting; on the weekends, they prowled the mountains. "One night I was tired and wore out and fell asleep in a pile of leaves somewhere back on a cliff and dreamed I was home in bed and was so comfortable. When someone came and woke me up and said, 'Let's go,' I was so disappointed, because I thought I was home in the bed. Right then, I thought there must be something better to chase than coons and bears. That's when I bought the car, and the following summer, Peggy and I started to date."

Two years later, on September 16, 1960, the couple was married at the home of Rev. Robert Cotton, the preacher at Massies Mill Presbyterian Church at that time. Clem laughed and said that Peggy's mother didn't have a lot of confidence in the man and said, "Well, I reckon he married them!"

The Lawhornes started out living with Peggy's parents, and their first child, Keith, was born there. They laughed at the memory of that night when Peggy went into labor and her mother suggested that instead of driving to the Lynchburg Hospital in their car, they should call Mr. Moore, from the funeral home in Roseland, who had an ambulance. It took him thirty minutes to get to the house, then

Peggy's parents, John and Lena Lawhorne; Lena's brother Willie in the background

in Amherst the ambulance had a flat tire. Luckily, they had time to spare, but at one point in the journey, Peggy's mother asked, "Mr. Moore, will this thing run any faster?" Mr. Moore replied, "I'm already going eighty now!"

By this time in the interview, we were all laughing. Just when I thought we had composed ourselves somewhat, Peggy added, "Oh, and when we got to the hospital, Mama discovered she had forgotten her teeth!" If that wasn't hilarious enough, Peggy said when their daughter, Wanda, was born, they decided to forgo the ambulance and drive their own truck. When Clem pulled into the emergency room, they looked in the back of the truck and realized that their dog had made the trip with them! In addition to their two children, today the Lawhornes have three grandchildren and two great-grandchildren.

Clem and Peggy stayed with Peggy's parents five years, then moved to a little cinder-block house down on Route 56, close to the Tye River. They moved to their present home at the foot of Cox's Creek in October 1966, three years before Hurricane Camille ripped through Nelson County, Virginia, on August 19, 1969, causing untold devastation. Odell Lawhorne was living in the cinder block house by that time, and Clem said the water got up to the ceiling during the flood and nearly washed away the house. Odell had gone out the back door and climbed to the top of a big oak tree, and the water rose so high that he almost drowned before the storm finally subsided the next morning.

Clem had left Morton Frozen Foods in May 1966 and found work closer to home at a plant at Piney River that made titanium dioxide, which was used as coating for refrigerators and stoves and in high-grade automobile paint. Clem was working the night Camille hit and recounted just how bad the weather got.

"I was working the eleven to seven shift and left the house about ten fifteen p.m. By then the rain was pouring down so hard I had to cut my headlights off a number of times and drive by the lightning just to see out the window. I couldn't tell where the road was, and if I would have gone in a ditch, it would have washed my car away. When I got to the plant, if I would have swam in

I wouldn't have gotten any wetter. It was only about a hundred yards from the car to the door, but I was completely soaked and had to pour water out of my shoes when I made it inside.

"At twelve thirty a.m., we saw the first pickup truck float over top of a six-foot chain link fence with two strands of barbed wire. We lost power, and, by then, there was four foot of water in the building where the motors were. The next morning, a woman who had washed away from her house the night before got caught in a pile of debris outside the plant. Some men were able to rescue her in a boat, but I thought about what would have happened to her if she hadn't washed up on that debris.

"I spent the night at the plant and left on foot the next morning around nine a.m. and hitched a ride part of the way home and ended up walking through the mountains the rest of the way. I made it back around one p.m. The road up Cox's Creek was washed out so deep that you could have set three boxcars side by side, and they would have been level with the road. The creek split in three prongs after a big tree fell down above Wilson and Flora Lawhorne's house which saved them from the water.

"The rocks piled up about six feet deep around Harmony Church, diverting the water around the church, or else it would have been gone. Houses that were closed up tight ended up being swept away, but the ones that had water flowing through them, even if they had seven foot of water inside, stood."

Peggy said that their house hadn't had any damage, but the flood washed out a web-wire fence and deposited an untold amount of rock and mud on the property.

When all was said and done, Hurricane Camille, which was classed as a Category 5 hurricane by the National Weather Service, dumped rain in excess of twenty-five inches within a five-hour period, destroying roads, more than one hundred bridges, and more than nine hundred buildings. Sadly, 114 people lost their lives, and thirty-seven remain missing. Camille was one of the most devastating natural disasters Virginia had ever experienced, and its effects on the land and the people of Nelson County continue to this day.

Clem left the Piney River plant in 1971. He worked for a few years building houses with John Campbell and a few years by himself doing remodeling before finding work in 1976 at the Virginia Fibers paper mill—that later became Grief Brothers mill—in Riverville. Clemon had planned on retiring at sixty-two after twenty-five years of service, but eight months before his birthday, he had an accident at the mill that left him unable to work, and he had to go out on disability. But the company had good insurance and kept Clem on through his numerous surgeries, right up until the time he was able to retire at sixty-five.

Before marriage and for a short while afterward, Peggy worked on an assembly line, sewing clothing at N&W Garment Factory and the Blue Buckle Company, both based in Lynchburg. When her children were older, she worked closer to home at Silver Creek Orchard, which later changed to Flippin/Seaman Orchard. After Bill Flippin retired, the same orchard became Silver Creek/Seaman Orchard. Peggy has worked there for twenty-eight years and continues to go in to help when they need it.

Clemon is a man of many talents, and when asked what he likes to do with his time, he laughs and says, "People ask me what my hobbies are, and sometimes I forget how many hobbies I've got."

The covered bridge that Clem built

In 1986, Clem built a beautiful covered bridge across Cox's Creek; it joins his upper homeplace with his son, Keith's, home, as well as Icem and Peggy Lawhorne's. Keith and many of Clem's neighbors, including Icem, helped with the construction.

Clem has also remodeled the inside of his family homeplace, and in 1998, he built a one-room cabin out of heart of cedar wood. In 2004, he built a wooden overshot waterwheel and is in the process of powering electricity from the wheel to the cabin. Clem is also an avid fan of antique cars, and he and Peggy can be seen cruising the roads in his bright red classic 1955 Chevy Bel Air, two-door hard-top with a 300-horsepower, three-speed automatic transmission. I smiled and asked if he still likes to go fast; Clem matched my smile and said, "Yeah, I like to try it out."

Clem's '55 Chevy

He and Peggy go to car shows together, and Clem enjoys going to Carlisle, Pennsylvania, to look at and admire what everybody else has. Both Lawhornes love bluegrass music and treat every-one at their annual pig roast to the tunes of the Little Mountain Boys band. And, of course, Clem is always cutting and splitting firewood—a never-ending task here in the mountains where most everyone heats with wood.

Clem and his classic car

When asked if he misses the old days, Clem said that there are things he still misses, but he wouldn't want to go back to all that hard work. "By the time we were ten, eleven, we were cutting timber with a crosscut saw. My older brother was about fourteen years old, and my dad let him take our mare and drag out the trees that were cut. He would tell my brother Sam and myself not to touch the horse's bridle because we were too little. We resented that and were always pulling pranks on him to get even.

"We even pulled pranks on our father, but after they were done, we all ended up laughing. My dad had a funny byword he always used when he got mad at something. He'd say, 'Gosh O Hemlocks, Holy Cripes!' We were always up to some mischief, and if I didn't get a switching at least every other day, I wasn't satisfied. My daddy never had to beat me because when he spoke, he meant what he said. But Mom kept these old willow switches, and you remember that old telephone commercial that said, 'Reach out and touch someone'? Well, she could sure reach out and touch us!

Clem with a respectable pile of firewood that he split

Clem and Peggy at their Cox's Creek home

"One day, I found where she hid those switches, and I stole them. The next day, I did some kind of mischief, and I can still see the expression on her face when she went to get the switches and couldn't find them. I waited a few days and hid them again, but she outsmarted me by having two bundles, and when I realized I was in trouble, I jumped out the end window of the house, but she caught me by the nape of my neck before I hit the ground, and I tell you one thing, by the time she turned me loose, it wasn't a laughing matter!"

The tape in my recorder stopped, and it was at this point that the official interview ended, but we continued to talk a little longer at the kitchen table. I thought what a pleasant way to spend an afternoon—talking with friends. When did that cease being the norm? We pulled on our coats and headed outside to take a few photos for the book. The one of Clem and Peggy is my favorite: two happy people, still in love and doing things together after fifty-two years of marriage. Thank you for such a great life story, and may God bless you both.

Lorean Painter

10

Lorean Falls Painter

Over the years that *Backroads* was published, Lorean Painter attended many of the reunions and special functions I covered for the newspaper. But I never had the pleasure of interviewing her individually during that time. Since all the stories in the three Backroads books were taken from the old newspaper articles, Lorean's life story was not featured. When I decided to write this fourth book, I chose to talk to the people I hadn't interviewed before, so that all the material would be fresh and interesting.

The day we talked, I learned that we have the same birthday, twenty-eight years apart. It also came out that she was the sister of Willard and Hunter Falls, a fact I hadn't known. It's not until you talk in detail to a person, instead of chatting about everyday things, that you begin to fit pieces into the puzzle of their life. Lorean's story is typical of women who were raised up in the mountains, then married and raised their own families with the values that were instilled in them as children. These values are still important, maybe even *more* important in today's society with all the distractions that seem to pull us in every direction. So it is with great honor that I present the memories of a very special lady that everyone in the area knows and loves.

Lorean Beatrice Falls was the seventh of eight children born to Azro Cora Falls, whose nickname was "Chug," and Katie Mildred

Campbell Falls. They lived in a home in the Mill Creek area of Montebello, Virginia. Like all the Falls children, Lorean was born at the family homeplace and delivered by a midwife. Lorean came into the world on October 5, 1919.

An early photo of Lorean's father, Chug Falls

Her siblings, in the order of their births, were: Willard, Elizabeth (Lizzie), Hunter, Harry (who died of rheumatic fever at age fifteen), Wilson, Elwood, and Maurie; Lorean was sandwiched in between Elwood and Maurie.

Their home, which was built by her mama's parents, had a kitchen, dining room, living room, bedrooms, and a path to the outhouse that was a "three-holer," consisting of two large holes and a little one for the smaller children.

Chug Falls was a subsistence farmer, like most men who lived in the mountains. He plowed his fields with horses and planted crops to feed both his family and his farm animals. The family kept horses, sheep, chickens, hogs, and cows. The horses did the heavy work, the sheep's wool was used to make warm clothing and batting for quilts, chickens produced eggs and meat, and hogs were butchered seven or eight at a time, usually between Thanksgiving and Christmas. Cows were milked each day, and butter was made from the cream in a wooden churn. Lorean said they also killed cattle for beef, which her

Lorean's parents, Chug and Katie Falls

The Chug Falls family

mother canned, preserving the meat. In the fall, they made apple butter, grape butter, and marmalade.

The Falls family was large, and it took every bit of what they could grow and put up to feed ten people throughout the year. Lorean laughed and added, "Six boys could sure eat a lot of food!"

Her mother cooked on a wood-burning cookstove, and the kitchen also had a fireplace with which to heat the home. In later years, the family put in a metal heating stove, providing a more constant and efficient heat source. Lorean recalled that the women of the family cooked three hot meals each day. Breakfast consisted of eggs, maybe some hog meat, biscuits and gravy, and perhaps some buckwheat cakes. They grew their own buckwheat along with the corn, and hauled the grain in cloth sacks on a horse drawn wagon to Osceola Mill in Vesuvius to be ground.

Elwood and Lorean as children

Lorean said that they never grew wheat, but her dad purchased five large wooden barrels of flour from the mill, and they used that to make bread. Hot bread was an everyday staple in a mountain home, and Lorean said enough fresh biscuits were made each morning, not just for breakfast but also to be packed in the children's school lunches. Supper was usually cooked vegetables, such as potatoes, brown beans, green beans, or anything else the garden produced during the season.

Lorean Falls Painter 161

As the boys got older and learned to drive, Lorean's father bought each of them a vehicle, and they took him where he needed to go. Up until that time, horse-drawn wagons were used to haul everything from grain to firewood to family members. Some of her brothers got jobs working on the "Skyline" (Blue Ridge Parkway) when it was being constructed, doing a variety of jobs to make a little money.

Her father and brothers hunted deer, bear, and squirrel, the meat providing variety in the family's diet. Staples such as sugar, salt, and coffee could be bought or bartered for at either Farris's or Robertson's store, which also carried clothing and shoes. "I remember my daddy walking to the store and buying our shoes, which he put into a feed sack and carried home on his back," said Lorean.

Lorean worked mostly indoors, doing "women's work," which she loved, and left the outside work to her father and six brothers. She remembers how they boiled water on the wood stove, carried it out, and poured it into large washtubs to wash clothes on a scrub board with homemade lye soap. The clean clothes were then rinsed and hung out to dry on a line. Back then, washday was always on a Monday, and Tuesday was ironing day. "I was crazy about ironing back then. We'd have six or eight flat irons heating up on the wood stove at one time, and we'd iron sheets, towels, and washcloths, as well as our clothes.

"Mama sewed all our clothes by hand. Some were made from printed feed sacks that had all kinds of colorful patterns on them. Why, I made some of my own daughter's dresses from those sacks. But I sewed on a foot-treadle sewing machine."

When asked what they did at Christmastime, Lorean said, "We didn't know what cutting a tree and decorating it was back then. We put plates out on the table, and Santy Claus would come and leave us a little candy or an orange. Mama would cook a big ham for Christmas dinner. Back then, you could go to the store with twenty dollars and buy a lot with it. Now you can't get too much for the same amount."

I asked if her family walked to relatives or neighboring people's homes for a meal during the holiday season as my husband's family did. Lorean said, "No, we lived too far from anyone's house, and at that time of year, the snow was deep, making it hard to walk anywhere."

The Falls children attended Mill Creek School, the closest one-room schoolhouse to their home, that had classes up to the seventh grade. Lorean remembers a Preacher Cunningham being one of her early teachers. Byrd Garnett was also a teacher there in later years, but she and Lorean were the same age and were good friends.

Lorean and her good friend, Byrd Garnett

Lorean walked to school with the three Bradley girls, Vivian, Ida, and Helen, neighbors who lived up the road. She also recalls the Fauber family, who lived over the ridge behind their home. Some of the teachers boarded with her family through the years. When asked about the distance they had to walk to get to school, Lorean said it was several miles. People nowadays don't walk like they used to. As an example, Lorean's son Jimmy, who keeps beagles, took them for some exercise at the homeplace. A friend was along one day, and they ended up at Mill Creek School. When Jimmy told the man that his mother used to walk to school there, the friend wanted to know why she hadn't just ridden the bus. Jimmy laughed and said, "Lord a mercy, there wasn't a bus back then!"

The school curriculum included spelling, arithmetic, reading, and history. Classes started around Labor Day and continued until late spring. For those wanting a few more years of education, the school at Montebello offered two years of high school. Lorean said that she'd started those two years, but because of the longer distance she had to walk alone, she decided to quit after just three weeks. She had chores to do before and after school, and the extra time it took to walk to Montebello was just too much on a little girl. Her older sister Lizzie attended the two years of high school there, but she stayed with another family during the week and came home on the weekends.

Mill Creek schoolchildren

The family primarily attended Mount Paran Baptist Church in Montebello but also the little Brethren Church close to where Homer Anderson had his store. They also went to services at South Mountain Chapel (Haines Chapel) where most of Lorean's people are buried.

Lorean said that she left home at twenty-five years of age, moving down to the Lofton area, and found employment at the Wayne Manufacturing Company in Waynesboro. She boarded with cousins of her future husband, Elwood Painter, whose family lived close by.

Elwood would walk over to visit, and soon the couple began courting; they married on November 3, 1943. Elwood was in the Army at the time and served in Italy during his military service. When he returned home, the Painters moved back in with Lorean's parents. Two of their three children were born at the homeplace: Bonnie Jane on May 3, 1946, and Jimmy Leon on June 5, 1948. At that time, her brother Willard and his wife, Vera, were living there as well, and Lorean laughed when she said, "It was getting a little crowded," so the decision was made to move back to the Lofton area, where they rented a little house and set up housekeeping near Week's Sandbank. Lorean and Elwood's last child, Janet Lee, was born there on November 9, 1953.

Lorean and her daughter Janet

Elwood started out working at Wayne Manufacturing. Later he went to work at DuPont in Waynesboro, where he stayed until he retired. Lorean's mother passed away first, then her dad came down and lived with them until his death. Willard and Vera moved back to the old homeplace up on the mountain and raised their four children there.

In the 1950s, the Painters hired John and Charlie Coffman to build them a home where Lorean continues to reside today. Her beloved husband, Elwood, passed away in 1999 after fifty-six years of marriage.

Lorean's children carefully watch over her and take care of all her needs. Bonnie married Richard Clements; they have two children and live in Buena Vista. Jimmy

Lorean and Elwood Painter on their fiftieth wedding anniversary

married Virginia, and they live right next to Lorean. Janet lives in Staunton with her husband, Roger Swisher, and they have one son.

The Painter family at the fiftieth anniversary celebration

Lorean's three children: Jimmy, Janet, and Bonnie

At ninety-three years of age, Lorean still has a positive atti-
tude and good humor about life. Looking around her tidy home,
I noticed a collection of beautiful dolls. When asked about them,
Lorean laughed and said, "I'm sorry I ever done that! Some I
bought, but mostly people started giving them to me."

As we talked, and the interview came to a close, I said, "How
have times changed since you were growing up?" Lorean responded
with several observations that give one pause.

"Kids stayed at home more. But I guess there wasn't nothing
else for them to do. I liked to work crossword puzzles, and Mama
and I would set up at night and quilt by lamplight. We kept sheep,
and if one would die, we would pick the wool off, wash it, and card
it, then use it for batting in between the quilt lining. We would
make quilts with patterns such as double wedding ring, friendship fan, Dutch girl, nine diamond, and flower basket. I believe
people were happier back then than they are now. They seemed
to be more sociable and have more time to visit. People made
time for one another. Mama and I would ride the horse, her riding

sidesaddle with me on the back, and spend the day with people quilting or just talking. Times have changed. The biggest thing is having electricity and indoor plumbing. We did have a big crank telephone in the kitchen wall that had a certain ring for each family."

Lorean finished up by saying that she missed living back in the mountains in some ways, but in other ways she likes what she has now.

Most every person I talked to while putting this book

Lorean at her ninetieth birthday party

together said the same thing. What they miss the most about living back in the mountains is the "quiet." May each of us take time from our busy lives to find a place of quiet to count our blessings . . . which are many.

Cousins Buck Harris and Lura Steele

11

Buck Harris and
Lura Coffey Steele

B uck and Lura are first cousins whom I met many years ago
at one of the Ramsey family reunions at the White Rock
homeplace along the north fork of the Tye River. Lura's
mother was Lora Burgess Ramsey Coffey, who was featured in my
second book, *Backroads: The Road to Chicken Holler.* Buck's mother
was Burgess's younger sister, Lena Jane Ramsey Harris Steele. Both
ladies, now deceased, will always hold a special place in my heart,
just as their children still do. I combined the cousins' story not only
to get more of their personal histories, but because they both share a
love of genealogy and are a great source of information about other
families who settled in the Blue Ridge Mountains in the 1700s.

I was first aware of Lura's ongoing interest in genealogy when
her nephew, Phillip Greene, saw her drive up one day and said,
"Here comes Aunt Lura with her bag of dead people!" She and
Buck always had their heads together at reunions, swapping facts,
trading photos, and fitting new pieces into the family puzzle. I
want to encourage people who would like to find out more about
their own family line but don't exactly know where to start. But
first, I'd like to share more of Buck and Lura's early family history
and their personal lives, because they intertwine and connect in
so many interesting ways.

The cousins' grandparents on their mother's side were William Marshall Ramsey and Serena Painter, but going back a little

farther is a series of twists and turns that one must concentrate on to stay focused.

John Painter married Mulvania Ramsey (Joshua Ramsey's daughter). There were three children born to the marriage, one of whom was a daughter named Serena. Mulvania died in childbirth along with her fourth baby. John then married Mary Elizabeth "Mollie" Hamilton (daughter of James Hamilton and Susan Harlow Hamilton). John and Mollie had four more children of their own before John died, bringing the total number of children to seven.

Mollie then married William Marshall Ramsey, Buck and Lura's grandfather. William and Mollie were living near the headwaters of the Pedlar River, in an area known as Oronoco, in Amherst County when the first of their six children was born. In 1897, they bought 134 acres and built a large home at the foot of Bald Mountain.

The William Ramsey homeplace on Bald Mountain

In 1906, William applied for a bank loan of three hundred dollars to buy a new Frick sawmill and a steam engine to power it. It became such a successful business that in two short years the loan was paid off. Between 1915 and 1917, the house caught fire; and William was injured when a large cabinet he was trying to carry downstairs fell on his leg. He was permanently crippled and never could work in the fields again. But he was industrious and learned to spin wool from his herd of sheep and crocheted socks, gloves, and hats for the family to wear during the cold winter months. When Mollie died, William was left with thirteen children to raise.

Serena and William Ramsey with their son Brainard standing behind them; twins Harry and Herman Bradley (sons of Dan and Mary Bradley) in front

William then applied for a marriage license to one of his older stepdaughters, Serena, who was no blood kin. The couple had ten children of their own: Sammy, Homer, Elmer, Lora Burgess, Ella, Bessie, Mary, Lina, Lena, and Brainard—plus William raised his son Don's child, Stanley—bringing the total to twenty-four children that William actually raised. In his will, William made provision for Stanley to have the same portion of property as his other children upon his death.

Buck recalled with a laugh one of the chores his mother, Lena, had to do as a child each morning was to light her father's pipe.

Hercy Coffey (1916)

Lura's mother, Burgess, had to bring him a pan of warm water, a wash-rag, and towel so that he could wash his face and hands, then she could dry him off.

Lura's mother, Lora Burgess, was born on April 28, 1902, and later married Hercy Coffey on April 3, 1921. They met while attending services at the White Rock Christian Church. When Burgess was in labor with her first child, Marjorie, she sent her husband up to the homeplace to fetch her mother, Serena, and bring her back. Gilbert Bryant rode with Hercy and they were both on horseback. It was January 11, 1922, and there was snow on the ground.

On the way, Serena had a fatal heart attack and fell off her horse to the ground. Gilbert laid his coat on the snow and the men placed Serena on it until they could ride to Ethna Seaman's house to get a ground sled to take her home. When Hercy got home, he was very evasive as to why Serena was not with him. Nearly a week went by before Burgess finally pinned down a family member and said, "You might just as well tell me, because I already know I'm never going to see my mother again."

At the time, Hercy and Burgess were living at the old Wallace place near Dowell's Ridge. They then moved to White Rock to the old Taylor cabin, and on December 24, 1922, their second

Eli Coffey family at Davis Creek (1910)

daughter, Lura, was born. Their last child, Lorine, was also born at the Taylor place on October 23, 1926. After that time, the family moved across the river to Hercy's parents' one-room log cabin that had been vacant since his family had moved to Waynesboro. Their privacy was short lived, however, because Hercy's parents, Eli and Fanny, and Eli's brother Tom moved in with them, as well as another brother, his wife, and two children.

Now twelve family members were living in a very tight space, plus one of the school teachers at White Rock was boarding with them. They divided

Fanny and Eli Coffey at the White Rock homeplace (1939)

Eli Coffey in later years

up the main room and the upstairs loft into small rooms so that everyone had their own, albeit tiny, space. Lura, with a laugh, could not remember where the school teacher slept; no one else wanted to speculate, so we left it.

Hercy owned and operated a sawmill, a gristmill, and a small store on the river; in 1933, construction was started for a home of their own. The new home was located behind Hercy's parents' cabin, and the family moved in permanently in 1934. It's the lovely place in which the girls were raised and called home until they married.

Lura said that as children, she and her two sisters did the standard chores around the house and helped their parents in the store, sawmill, and gristmill. She remembers removing slabs of wood and sawdust and stacking the finished lumber that their father had cut at the mill. At twelve years of age, they waited on folks who came to their store to buy something. Many times, family members would be away from the counter doing something else and people would holler to let them know they were there.

She said that back then, coffee was five cents a pound, baking soda, two cents. They sold coffee beans in fifty-pound bags; it could be ground there or taken home and ground in the individual grinders that most people kept in their kitchens. Hercy bought items from Blue Ridge Wholesale Company in Lexington, Virginia, and brought them back to sell from his store. Everything from coffee, sugar, salt, baking powder, and baking soda to candy, thread, canned goods, and hundred-pound sacks of all types of beans were bought and resold at Coffey's Store in White Rock. Lura said that Clarence Coffey also ran a store and mill farther up the North Fork on Durham's Run.

Lura and her sisters could also grind people's corn at the gristmill when their parents were gone, and Lura recalled a family that came down from Meadow Mountain (Love) with enormous sacks of corn piled high on their mules. It would take about half a day to grind the corn, so until they were ready to leave, the men would put the mules inside a little corral the Coffeys kept for their cows.

My husband, Billy, said that there was a good chance those

Burgess at their store with three of her grandchildren: Bobby, Ann, and baby Bonnie (1952)

men with the mules were his great uncles, Ellis and Royal Everitt, who lived in Chicken Holler and would have used the old connecting road from Squaremouth Rocks down to Hercy Coffey's mill.

Lura, along with her two sisters, attended the White Rock School. Unlike for many of the other mountain kids, their walk to school was a short one; just across the river from their home. Remembering some of her early teachers, Lura said that the first was a Shields girl. Then came Elva Coffey of Coffeytown, Robert Hill of Tyro, Ira Campbell, a Miss Jones from Massies Mill who taught for two years, and Hallie Cage from Keysville who taught two or three years. Lura said that Hallie boarded with Mr. Marshall Fitzgerald, and the two men boarded with Lee Fitzgerald, both of whom had large houses down the North Fork Road. Lura

Hercy Coffey's gristmill at White Rock

went the required seven grades at White Rock and continued to attend school for several years afterward, "Because I liked to go and have a good time."

When I asked about courting, she reeled off a list of boys' names whom she'd casually dated. At that time, dating con-

Schoolchildren from White Rock (1930)

White Rock School pupils (1940); Lura, age seventeen, is sitting at the front

sisted of the boys coming to the house and just talking or making some music and singing together. She said that on the weekends, it was nothing for their house to be filled with ten or more young people. Her cousin, Elwood Taylor, played the guitar, and he came every night after supper to play and sing. "Glenn Allen would also come to play music with Elwood, and, at the time, he was sweet on my sister, Lorine, and Elwood was sweet on Glenn's sister, Louise, so that's all I heard about . . .

Cousins Elwood and Lura (1942)

Lura and Johnny on their wedding day
(October 20, 1947)

Glenn and Louise, Glenn and Louise," laughed Lura.

"When Aunt Lena moved to Steele's Tavern, I went to stay with her. I was about twenty-two years old at the time, and I got a job at DuPont in Waynesboro where Lena was working. There was a bus that took the people to DuPont each day, and Aunt Lena and I rode it together. About that time, I met Johnny Rush Steele when he returned home from the Army. His family was one of the founders of Steeles Tavern."

After a few years' courtship, the couple married on October 20, 1947, at Old Providence Presbyterian Church; Rev. Grier officiated the service. Their first child, Bobby, was born at the Lexington Hospital on June 8, 1948. Buck remembered riding with Johnny down to the hospital to see Lura and the new baby. At that time, Lura and Johnny were still living upstairs in the large home at Steeles Tavern along with Glenn and Lorine, who had married and set up housekeeping in the two upstairs rooms adjoining Lura and Johnny's.

By the time the Steeles' daughter Ann was born on October 20, 1949, they had moved to the old Zink home near Mount Joy Church on Route 608. Bonnie was born next, on March 25, 1951. Sadly, Bonnie passed away from leukemia when she was twenty-six years old, leaving her husband, Harold Craig, a widower at a very young age.

The Johnny Steele family: Ann, Bonnie, Bobby, Lura, and Johnny (1966)

Lura said that her husband drove a truck during the early years of their marriage, then later got a job at the Celanese factory in Verona—where they made all types of cloth—and then at the new Westinghouse plant, also based in Verona.

In 1951, the family moved to Spottswood to a home built around the 1870s, and that's where the children were raised and called "home." In the years following, Johnny became ill and took a medical retirement from his job; he passed away in 1973. Lura was fifty years old, Johnny, fifty-two. Lura started working at the Spottswood post office as an assistant to the acting postmaster, Viney Campbell, in 1968 and continued there for twenty years.

The old home where Lura lived was getting in need of a lot of repairs, so it was torn down; in 1982, Lura moved to a new home on the same property, where she continues to reside. At present, besides her two children, Lura now has two grandchildren and six great-grandchildren. She has many interests that include working at the local food bank and making colorful quilts. But her passion has been and continues to be working on family genealogy.

Buck's mother, Lena Jane Ramsey, was born on March 2, 1907. After Lena's mother, Serena, died in 1922, fifteen-year-old Lena went to live with her half-brother, Christian, and his wife, who were living in Lofton, Virginia. Later, Lena met and fell in love with Frank Harris, who was also from Lofton, and they married in September 1928.

Frank bought fifty-seven acres and a new home from Mike Bartley for the sum of three hundred dollars. The house was located in Pikin, across the railroad tracks and up Spy Creek. When asked when and where he was born, Buck replied, "February 24, 1932, in Pikin, USA." Pikin, like Love, is more or less a bump in the road; it is

Lura with some of her colorful handmade quilts

Buck's father, Frank Newton Harris

located off Route 608 near Vesuvius, Virginia. Buck remembers going to the Pikin School; on the first day when the teacher asked his mother what his name was, she replied, "Buck." "When they pressed her for my given name, Mother at that moment couldn't remember it. You know Mother!"

Buck, whose real name is Lynden Thomas, can't recall where the nickname came from, but he said that he's always been stuck with it. He went to the Pikin

School for three years and remembers his first teacher being Elizabeth Hayes. Inez Brooks was the woman who made them lunch
each day, and Buck said that she cooked the best food. "But she
always cooked lima
or great northern
beans six days out of
five!" Pikin School
closed in 1939, so
he finished up at the
Spottswood School,
graduating from the
eleventh grade in
1949 at age seven-
teen.

Frank Harris was a
carpenter who loved
his family, but he suf-
fered from high blood
pressure and died at
age forty-nine from a
cerebral hemorrhage.
Buck was eleven at
the time, his brother,
Buddy (born January
4, 1930), was thir-
teen, and his sister,

Lena Steele

Margaret (born March 23, 1928), was fifteen. Before their father
died, Lena had found work at the DuPont plant in Waynesboro,
and the family had moved from Pikin to Spottswood, making it
easier for his mom to find a ride to work. After Frank's death, they
moved to the large house at Steeles Tavern, where many of their
other family members ended up living as well, and in June 1953,
Lena married William P. Steele.

Buck remembers that at fourteen years of age, he would get off
the bus after school and work a job at Merle Davis's service station.
After graduation, Buck spent the three summer months working

with Gordon Patterson, the station agent at the Lyndhurst train depot. Gordon taught him the ropes of being a telegraph operator, and, at the end of the summer, Buck went to Roanoke to take the test. He did well, and they said that if he'd put down on the application that he was eighteen, they'd hire him tomorrow. Buck fibbed a little and found himself on the Norfolk and Western Railroad from Winston/Salem, North Carolina, to Hagerstown, Maryland.

The stations were numerous, about every five miles apart. "I remember there was one at Cold Spring, Vesuvius, Lofton, Stuarts Draft, Crimora, and beyond. I did that until 1950, when I enlisted in the Air Force. I was shipped to the Philippines and Korea towards the end of the war. They said if you were in Korea longer than six months, you could get discharged. I came home and went back to being a telegraph operator but found all the stations had closed in the three years I had been gone."

From 1953 until 1956, Buck continued to work for the Norfolk and Western Railroad in the Roanoke division office as a telegraph operator at night, while attending Roanoke College during the day. Being a curious adventurist, and wanting to get in some great fishing and hunting in Alaska, he decided to resign from the railroad and transfer his credits from Roanoke College to the University of Alaska to finish up his premedical education.

In the fall of 1956, the government was just finishing up building the Distant Early Warning (DEW) Line, a radar network from the western side of Alaska, across Alaska, Canada, and Greenland to the eastern side of Iceland. In seeking a part-time job to assist with his college fees, Buck applied for a job with the construction contractor in Fairbanks, Alaska, that was building the DEW Line. This resulted in a longtime commitment—more than thirty years—between the ITT Corporation and Buck. The radar stations were constructed about every ninety miles from west to east and along the Arctic Ocean; there were thirty-two stations to start with, all hundreds of miles north of the Arctic Circle.

Buck started as a transportation specialist in 1956 and when he retired in 1988, he was the project manager and responsible for the entire system. His relationship with the ITT Corporation allowed him to come and go—from one project to another or to and from anywhere within the corporation. This gave him opportunities to work on the space program in California, from Gemini through the Apollo missions; the Ballistic Missile Early Warning System (BMEWS) in Alaska, Greenland, and England; and the North Atlantic Treaty Organization (NATO) radio system in Iceland, Scotland, Denmark, and various British Isles. It even gave him the opportunity to return to Virginia and marry the love of his life, Barbara Kay Armstrong of Greenville, on February 8, 1964.

Buck also owned and operated a saw mill in Nelson County with his uncle B. T. Ramsey and was employed for a few years as a Virginia state game warden. But the call of the North was

Buck and Barbara on their wedding day (February 8, 1964)

always there. Buck and his family were able to live in various areas of the country and travel throughout the world. He and his family have lived in Iceland, Alaska, California, and Colorado, as well as in Virginia. He and Barbara were able to travel throughout the British Isles, plus the Scandinavian countries of Denmark, Sweden, and Norway, following Buck's work.

The Harrises had two children: Tammy, who now lives in Roanoke; and Lynden, who is in Atlanta, Georgia. At present, Buck has three grandchildren.

Buck's beloved wife, Barbara, passed away in September 2010; in 2011, Buck made the move to a smaller apartment in Staunton so that he wouldn't have the upkeep of a large home. He shares his apartment with his little poodle, Katie, who keeps him entertained and is a lot of company for him. He has always enjoyed the sports of fishing and golf and, like his cousin Lura, he loves genealogy.

Buck said he got his start in genealogy in 1954 when he sat down with his aunts Burgess and Ella and began asking questions. But it wasn't until his retirement in 1988 that he went full bore into genealogy.

Lura began in 1982 when she met a distant relative (Ruth Coffman), who called to ask if Lura's mother would go across the mountain to show her where all the old people lived up and down the north fork of the Tye River. Ruth also wanted to find and record the graves in the old mountain cemeteries in the same area. Lura went along and said they visited all those places and had a good time talking. About a week later, Ruth was back again, and they started going to the court houses and libraries in Lovingston, Charlottesville, and Lynchburg. Lura told us that from 1982 until about two years ago, she and Ruth attended all the Fitzgerald reunions that were held in the mountains.

Both Buck and Lura are quick to add that the absolute best part of their work is the people they have come in contact with who share the same passion. They named Carol Hite Harlow, Shirley Houck, Oscar Nuckolls, Wayne Coffey, Hilda Austin, Kenny Allen, and many others. Buck recalls the time one summer that they all went to identify and inventory thirty-seven cemeteries in a seven-mile radius around Montebello. Families names like Taylor, Campbell, Phillips, Fitzgerald, Allen, Bradley, Coffey, Painter, Hamilton, Harris, and Ramsey were found. Buck added that once you get past the Ramseys, most of their descendants are Campbells, who were Scots/Irish. The Coffey side of the family came to the Davis Creek area around 1744.

Both Lura and Buck encourage anyone who wants to get started in documenting their heritage to first get a computer, not only to maintain the record but to do the online research. One can buy a rebuilt used computer of sufficient size to accommodate all your needs for about three hundred dollars. A "family tree program" can be downloaded from the LDS library in Salt Lake City for free, or you can purchase a FTM program for less than fifty dollars. If you are not computer literate, almost all of the local libraries have a genealogy library that teach free classes on researching and recording your family history. Each library also has its own genealogy section, and

Buck's paternal great-grandparents,
James Franklin Harris and Ozello Crist Harris

The Bradley family at the turn of the century

each county has a Historical Society, both of which are excellent sources of information.

Once you get proficient with the use of a computer, there are two great websites you will want to use: www.familysearch.com gives you free access to the LDS (Mormon) library in Salt Lake City that has millions of records for your family search; and www. ancestry.com can be accessed free for fourteen days at a time. Here you may find your family tree already completed by an unknown relative and available for free download. Visiting county court houses is essential for maintaining accuracy. Household census records have been kept since the 1780s, reported every ten years by heads of household until 1850; since then, every person has been recorded.

DNA testing is now available to classify individuals into clans, then into family groups; but the process is expensive and still only gives assurances up to seven generations.

The biggest kick you may get during research is the day you knock down a brick wall and find the details on your great-great-grandfather that you've been searching years for without success. That makes all the effort worthwhile. Courthouses also have records of written wills and property deeds.

Lura said that you would be surprised what you can find recorded in a deed: when children were born, their names, where a family's land was located, who their neighbors were. Buck and Lura say that oral history is the most reliable, because years ago that's all people had to work with—stories that were handed down from generation to generation and old photos with names and dates written on the back. Both cousins got a great deal of information from their mothers, so now is the time to talk to the elders in your own family before they are gone and take the history with them to the grave.

You can also search old obituaries, marriage licenses, and birth/death certificates. Genealogy is a highly recommended hobby for the younger generations, and Buck and Lura both say that it's a great thing to find information from written records, then have an older person validate the facts so that you know what you've found is correct.

Buck, Margaret, and Buddy with their mother, Lena

And so the interview came to a close. As we sat around the kitchen table finishing up and just chatting the afternoon away, I asked the same question I always end up asking these dear people that I know and love: "Name something you miss about living back up in the mountains when you were growing up."

Buck smiled at a memory that was as fresh today as it was when it happened. "During the summer months, most every night after supper, the family and perhaps a neighbor or two would gather on the porch to discuss their activities of the day and build a 'gnat smoke.'"

When I inquired what a gnat smoke was, both he and Lura said, "You take some small dried sticks and place them in a metal can and start a fire in the can. When it gets going good, pull some green grass and weeds and put [them] on top of the fire. A great smoke would come forth and keep the gnats away better than any spray product you can buy today." Buck continued, "The older folks would sit or rock on the porch; perhaps some chewing tobacco or just relaxing by whittling on a stick. When night came, the kids would be out in the yard catching fireflies, listening to the talk of their elders."

It was a peaceful time. A time to unwind from the day's physical labors. A time to catch up and visit with your family or neighbors. No telephones to interrupt conversation. No hurry. Mountain time . . .

Janie and David Coffey (Coffeytown)

Mary and Frances Cash

12

Frances and Mary Cash

I have to admit, these two women hold a very special place in my heart. They are very private people, and for that reason I have never given them any exposure in either *Backroads* newspaper or the three Backroads books. But as the plans for *Appalachian Heart* began to come together, I wanted very much to include them in this final tribute to the mountain people I know best.

I had always heard about the Cash sisters but never had the pleasure of meeting them personally until my husband, Billy, took the pastorship of Mount Paran Baptist Church in Montebello. Frances and Mary would come to the homecoming service, revivals, and always the Christmas program in December. They always referred to me as "The Preacher's Woman," which delighted the daylights out of me. They were the most unique people I'd ever met, and over the years I came to know and love them deeply.

I took their photos and gave them copies, and I was honored when I saw many of the pictures framed and hanging on the walls of their home. But I never published any for fear of infringing on their privacy. When they both agreed to let me interview them for this book, and Frances said I could use the photos, my heart couldn't contain the joy I felt.

I have wonderful memories of these ladies. One I will always treasure was the time Billy and I walked with them back to their

Mary and Frances with Billy Coffey at a Mount Paran homecoming

homeplace. It was sometime in late winter; snow and ice were still on the ground. We were supposed to get a key to unlock the gate at the top of the mountain, but we never connected with the man who was to lend it to us. Frances volunteered that it wasn't that far to walk, so we began a downhill descent to where they'd spent most of their lives. We slipped and slid our way down to the Cash homeplace, and I took a multitude of photos.

The sisters suggested that we walk down to their grandparents' cabin, and, once again, I took quite a few pictures. Suddenly the abandoned cabins and outbuildings took on a life of their own as we heard the stories of growing up there, seeing what it must have been like through the sisters' eyes. We went to the remains of their Uncle Joe's home, then on to Dr. Bruce's cabin and the beautiful clear-blue pond on his property. Dr. Bruce, a retired dentist from Stuarts Draft, bought the property and built a get-away place among the mountain people; he offered free dental services to any of them who needed it.

By this time, it was getting long in the afternoon, and I knew we had an uphill climb back to our vehicle. The women had no intention of stopping and wanted to know if we'd like to walk down yet another ridge to an Indian den, where it was reported that Native Americans used to camp. Since the sun was slowly sinking over the mountain, we declined, knowing that in about an hour it would be dark.

I whispered to Billy that he should take the lead back, stopping often to rest; not for Frances and Mary—these women were like mountain goats, climbing steadily, never winding—but for *me*, who was huffing and puffing like a train. We made it back before dark, and the sisters chatted away in the back seat on the trip down the mountain, telling us who lived where. I never forgot the fun we had that day.

Another memory I'll carry in my heart was the time I was out delivering *Backroads* newspapers at the Montebello Store and ran into Frances and Mary, sitting on a stack of cat- and dog-food bags they had piled on the floor and sipping a Mountain Dew. I asked if they wanted a ride home, and, as they conferred, I talked to Madeline Grant, the proprietress of the store. The sisters said yes, and we began carrying out the bags of food to put in the trunk of the car.

Oh, yes, about the car. At that time I was driving a 1968 bright red Ford Fairlane convertible, and on that warm summer day, the top was down. Although I didn't have my camera handy, in my memory I will never forget the picture of Frances and Mary sitting in the back seat, gray hair flying in the wind as we rounded the curves toward their home. It was a priceless gift that can never be duplicated and one I will always treasure.

At eighty-two and seventy-one years, respectively, Frances and Mary Cash, known simply as "The Sisters," are two of the toughest mountain women I have ever known. They were brought up that way and have continued to live the same lifestyle throughout their 153 combined years.

The Cash sisters came from hearty stock with Campbell, Maddox, Cash, and Mays ancestral names in their blood. Their paternal grandparents were Stanley Cash and Lydia Bell Mays Cash. On the maternal side were grandparents Lewis Campbell and Millie Maddox Campbell. The Campbell/Mays/Maddox side of the family lived down in Piney River, close to Shoe Creek. The Cashes lived high up in the Blue Ridge Mountains in a place aptly named "Cashtown," up a steep, winding dirt road that led to Crabtree Meadows at the head of Crabtree Falls, which is the tallest waterfall east of the Mississippi.

The Bingham Mays family; Lydia Bell Mays (the sisters' grandmother) on the far left

The sisters' father was Cyrus Cash, son of Stanley and Lydia Cash, and their mother was Judith Frances Campbell, daughter of Lewis and Millie Campbell. Cyrus and his sister Annie were raised up in a large, two-story log cabin in Cashtown; Judith was raised up in her parents' Piney River home. When Judith and Cyrus married, Judith bought seventy-five acres adjoining her in-laws' cabin and the old schoolhouse that Cyrus had attended as a child. The couple converted the school into a home and raised their ten children there.

Frances, who was born on February 26, 1930, named her nine siblings: "Dutch" (whose real name was Grant), Roy, Lucy, Hercy,

The Stanley Cash homeplace

Frances and Mary standing at their paternal grandparents' old home

John, Ray, Lester, Flossie, and Mary, who was born on September 29, 1941. Dutch, Roy, and Lucy were born in Piney River, and the rest were born either at their schoolhouse home or their grandparents' cabin. The sisters' grandmother Lydia (whom they refer to as "Granny Let") was the midwife who delivered all the children except Mary. Gracie Cash, who lived in a home on the Crabtree Falls road, delivered Mary. Of the ten children, four never married: Dutch, Lester, Frances, and Mary.

The extended Cash family, as well as their Campbell cousins (Owen, Maybelle, and Jimmy), lived in a very isolated part of the mountains and kept mostly to themselves. They were self-sufficient, growing and raising everything they needed to survive. Frances relates, "Our kin people had some hard living. We've heard people say they had a hard life growing up, but compared to us, they had an easy life."

The Cyrus Cash homeplace where Frances and Mary grew up

Frances also said that as children, they didn't get much education. The closest school was across the ridge on Nettle Mountain, quite a distance away. "We didn't have shoes," said Frances. "We walked in our bare feet summer and winter. The snow was so deep in the winter that we halfway froze to death trying to get to school, so we just quit going." One of the teachers there, Marie Seaman, gave Lucy a pair of little slippers one time, but they were too big for her to wear. The first pair of shoes that Frances remembers getting was given to her by Chester Coffey. The shoes were hand-me-downs that didn't quite fit, but she said that she was glad to get any kind of shoe.

Their daddy farmed a little and cut wood, and in the fall he was a crew boss for the people picking apples at the various orchards. He was also very adept at making sturdy woven baskets from splits he'd make from white oak trees. Frances said that he would look for a tree that was free of knots, then he'd cut it in half, then fourths, etc., until he had a small section he could handle and rip the splits off with his pocket knife. He'd shave them down smooth, and when he was ready to make a basket, he'd soak the splits in water to make them pliable and easier to weave.

His mother and grandmother had taught him the art of basketmaking, and the sisters said that people came from near and far to buy them. He never sold them at the various stores near Montebello, but folks knew he did quality work and were willing to make the long trip up the mountain to purchase one. He made everything from small egg baskets to rectangular garden baskets, round baskets in various sizes to large hampers. His work was

Frances holding one of her father's white oak baskets that they still use

Close-up of one of Cyrus Cash's baskets

generational, meaning that the vessels would last from one generation to another and stood up to constant use.

Frances is shown holding one of the last baskets that their father made, which they were using to carry in green beans from their garden. If you look closely, you can see the fine patina on wood that has seen many years of use. Mary also learned basketry from her dad and became very good at it; she made quite a few herself. Frances laughed and said that her brother Dutch tried his hand at it, but the ones he made were too small and round and ended up looking like a horse muzzle.

I asked Frances if she ever made baskets, and it was my turn to laugh when she said, "No, I didn't have time. I was so busy in the timber business I didn't have time to get my breath hardly." I can personally vouch for Frances's love of timbering. For as long as I've known her, she's been out by their never-ending woodpile with either a saw or an axe in her hand. In earlier years, she'd used a crosscut saw to down trees, but her brother-in-law Robert Hite finally got her a used Homelite chain saw, and it opened up a whole new world of timbering for Frances.

"Why I could cut trees this big [makes a big circle with her arms]. I timbered saw logs, pulp wood, and locust posts that I cut in half."

Bill Flippin once asked Frances who had taught her to cut posts, and she told him, "I learned it by myself. He'd [Bill] buy everyone I cut and said I was the toughest post buster he'd ever seen." When she finally wore out the Homelite, she purchased a new Stihl saw that she continues to use to this day. But she still splits rounds of wood with an axe. I asked what she did if the axe got stuck in the wood, and Frances replied, "Why, I'd knock it out! I use a steel wedge and a wooden 'glut'; that's all you need." She confessed that as a young girl, she was out chopping wood one day, and "I chopped my foot but didn't tell nobody."

Another source of income for the mountain people was picking apples in the fall. Frances would often ride to the orchards with her brother-in-law Robert, who was a labor hauler, while Mary stayed home with their mother. Frances remembers the first time she met Johnny Coffey (my first neighbor here in Love and a well-known orchard man).

"He like to tickled me to death . . . the way he called everybody 'Son.' He was back on Dry Branch, and he hired me to pick apples. They had one tree that was surrounded by a wire fence, and nobody wanted to climb over that wire fence. I was skinny and light, and I walked that ladder bridge and climbed on up into the tree. I was about seventeen or eighteen years old and was an adventurer! Johnny bragged on me after that and said I was a better picker than all the Allen boys put together. Whatever he told me to do, I'd do it. He could always count on me."

Gathering enough firewood to heat the house and stoke the cookstove was an ongoing project, and the sisters recall a snowy winter day when they had one of the horses hooked to a ground sled piled high with firewood; they came down the steep hill to their home riding on the back, going at a good clip. One of their brothers told them to stop or he'd tell their daddy, but Frances yelled back, "No danger, no danger," as they sped home without incident.

In addition to their home, the Cash family also had the necessary outbuildings that went along with a mountain farm: a spring house to keep milk and butter cold, a ground house (root cellar) where apples and hog meat was kept, a place for the chickens (who provided eggs and meat), and three stables (two for their horses and a large one for the cows). When asked how many horses they had, a count of four was made: Bob, Jeff, Prince, and Bessie. And even after all these years, Frances could still remember the names of all seventeen cows: Dot, Daisy, Blackie, Rosie, Spot . . . etc.

Dot was Frances's first cow, whom she milked two-handed style into a bucket. The whole time she was being milked, Dot would affectionately lick Frances's back. The milk was then poured into two-gallon jars and put in the springhouse to keep cool. From the rich cream, butter was made in wooden or stone churns; Frances said that this was a hot job in the summertime. They also made clabbered milk (a thick substance formed when milk was left to sour); that was my husband, Billy's, favorite.

The garden was extensive, and a large number of vegetables— potatoes, beans, corn, cucumbers, tomatoes, and cabbages—were grown to feed the big family. Potatoes and cabbages were buried in the ground over the winter and would keep until spring. Dried corn was shelled and taken to either Charlie Robertson or Ernest Grant's mill to be ground into meal. When money for coffee beans was scarce, cornmeal was put on the stove and parched (burnt brown), then put in a grinder to make a substitute drink that Frances said made "pretty good coffee."

When the weather turned colder, the family butchered hogs and cured the meat. Cyrus and his sons fished the streams for native trout and hunted for squirrel, deer, and bear. When asked if she ate bear meat, Frances wrinkled up her nose and offered that Mary does. "I won't eat bear because it looks too much like a German police dog! I never have eaten it . . . that, and oysters." I laughed and told her she's missed out on two delicious meats. I could tell by her face that she was unconvinced.

The family had no vehicle, so trips to visit relatives or the country stores in Montebello were made on foot with a sack to carry necessities back home in. The sisters said that they walked out on the Crabtree road, but their grandfather Stanley was over ninety years old and still walked out of the mountains "between the rocks." When I questioned this phrase, I was told it referred to taking the rocky path across Spy Rock, a shortcut that shaved time and distance off the trip but was much more treacherous.

As children, the sisters said that they didn't have any store-bought toys to play with, but they fashioned "play pretties" out of rocks, sticks, and oatmeal boxes. Christmas was celebrated by visiting with relatives who lived close by. "We'd go to our grand-parents' house, and Granny Let would play the organ, and we'd sing songs together. We never put up a tree in the house, but we'd get an orange, some nuts, and a little candy for Christmas."

Frances and Mary with their first cousin Maybelle Campbell

Frances said that a lot of the time, she'd walk down to her grandparents' cabin and spend time with them. She stayed for two months one time when her Granny Let was ill, and one night her granddaddy Stanley put too much dry wood in the stove and caused a chimney fire. Frances said there were a few feet of snow on the ground, and they had to keep running out to the spring to bring in buckets of water to try to put the fire out. She said that the fire sounded like the roar of a freight train, and she was sure that the house would burn down before they could put it out.

"Granddaddy crawled up on the roof and poured water down the chimney, and I climbed into the loft and threw water on the flue. I stayed up all night thinking it would start up again and never closed my eyes."

When the family attended church, they walked out to Mount Paran Baptist Church at the head of Irish Creek, where they still are members. They have family buried in the church cemetery, as well as Churchville and over at the Campbell/Cash graveyard located on their cousins' property.

As the children grew up, five of the boys got jobs at Klotz Brothers' Junkyard in Staunton, and many of them moved to the town permanently. One by one they left home, and six out of the ten married. Dutch, Frances, Lester, and Mary remained single their whole lives. As their parents aged, they eventually went to live with Lucy near Staunton and remained with her until their deaths. Dutch, Frances, and Mary continued to live back at the mountain homeplace, but life was much harder for just the three of them. They still had no electricity, phone service, or indoor plumbing, much less a vehicle to take them where they needed to go. They continued to make the eight- or nine-mile trip to the Montebello store on foot, carrying staples back home in a sack, just as their father had years before.

Winters were harsh and snowfalls were deep. Frances and Mary tell stories that seem unbelievable, except for the fact that we know they are true. Like the times they literally shoveled their way out to the main road with nothing but a snow "scoop." Frances said it took them two full days to cover a distance of about four miles. They would shovel until about one o'clock in the morning and come home bone tired, only to start again the next morning. At the time, Frances would have been about sixty years old and Mary, forty-nine.

The sisters tell of an icy winter day when they walked out to the store; before they could return home, the springs that ran over the road had frozen solid, making it impossible to cross. They had to hack the ice away with an axe to get enough footing to cross the road safely. They said it took them to way up in the middle of the night to get home. And Frances said it took one whole day for her to sharpen her axe head after the incident.

But if the sisters were tough, they were also inventive. They would pound horseshoe nails through the soles of their boots, cut them off and file them down to a point. In this way, they could walk on the snow and ice and never slip. It is said that necessity is the mother of invention, and the mountain people had plenty of necessities. I always liked the little ditty I learned when I moved here:

Use it up, wear it out
Make it do, or do without

These words could not be truer for the native mountain people, who used whatever they had, patched clothing until it was bare, then turned around and cut up what was left to make quilt pieces; they made do with the little they possessed with no thought of buying something new because they had no money anyway. And, more often than not, the families did without.

Twenty-two years ago, the decision was made for the Cash sisters to move from their Cashtown homeplace into a new little cottage built for them by Wilson and Madeline Grant. They have lived there ever since, still preferring to walk down through the woods the two miles to the same store they have done business with for many years. They still raise a big garden and keep a flock of Leghorn chickens. Mary loves her kitties and has an abundance of them, while Frances keeps four dogs.

They are both still splitting firewood and hauling it to the house in Mary's wooden wagon. They both agree that the house where they now live is easier to keep and closer to what they need, and there certainly isn't as much snow to shovel. In fact, the kind men of Montebello make sure they are well plowed out whenever the snow falls. Dutch moved off the mountain and lived with his sisters for four or five years before being confined to a nursing home then finally passing away. Six of the original Cash siblings are still living: Frances and Mary, their sister Lucy, and brothers Hercy, John, and Lester.

As our talk wound down, I asked Frances if she sometimes missed living back in Cashtown. "Yes, I miss the old ways. It was quiet back there in the mountains. All you heard was the whip-poorwill, whippoorwill, whippoorwill, and watch as that bird would get on the ash pile to dust his feathers. We could hear the cowbells tinkling up on the mountain. The ones on my cows had a 'tinky-tinky' sound . . . different than the others. Yes, I'm still walking. Still bustin' up wood. No, I don't never give up."

Ashton and Shield Critzer (Afton)

Icem Lawhorne of Cox's Creek

13

Icem Lawhorne

We met Icem and his wife Peggy years ago and have attended their annual July pig roast held at their home at the head of Cox's Creek. The view of Three Ridges Mountain from their property is spectacular and one I'm sure they never tire of, living high on the mountain completely surrounded by the tall ridges looming above them.

Billy and I have always been amused at Icem's statement about himself when he says, "Everyone living on Cox's Creek is mean.

View of Three Ridges Mountain from Icem's house

And the higher up the creek you go, the meaner they get. I live in the last house at the top!" But we've found his words contrary to the man, and I was excited with his answer of "yes" when asked whether he would let me interview him for *Appalachian Heart*.

If you are reading this book in 2013, Icem will be approaching his ninety-second year of living. He belies his age by a good thirty years and is the strongest man for his age I have ever known. There is no excess fat on his frame, and his muscles are taut from roaming the steep mountains where he was born and maintaining a very active lifestyle. The day I called Peggy to set up a time for the interview, I could hear a chain saw in the background, buzzing away. Peggy said that it was her husband, cutting up the laps from a tree that had recently fallen onto the house during a windstorm. The sawing continued through the whole length of our conversation—and long after we stopped, I'm sure.

We drove to their home on the coldest January day of 2013 and were instantly warmed by their wood stove and the Lawhornes' welcoming spirit. For the next three hours, we talked, laughed, and listened to incredible stories of life in the mountains from a genuine mountain man. I'm sure, as readers, you will enjoy them, too.

We settled in and began the interview by my asking Icem (pronounced EYE-sum) if he had always lived on Cox's Creek. He indicated that many generations of Lawhornes came before him on the creek, and Peggy, who has a vast knowledge of local history, said that the first family members settled in this particular area in the late 1700s; by 1850, they were well established up and down Cox's Creek. The Lawhornes have their roots in Wales, but the name is known all over the world.

Years ago, Icem and Peggy visited Wales and found a castle with the Lawhorne name. We all laughed when she said there was no doubt as to the family originating there because of the number of rocks in the soil. Anyone living in our part of the Blue Ridge knows the abundance of rocks we contend with day in and day out. When the Lawhorne ancestors came to America, no doubt they were looking for a place that reminded them of home. This was it, at least as far as the land was concerned.

Icem was the eighth of nine children born to Marcellus and Frances Lawhorne. His siblings were: Ada, Sally, Viney, Idell, Daniel, Mary, Queenetta, and Christy. Icem was born on October 26, 1921, and while he was still a young child, the family moved from the homeplace at the head of Maury Hollow to a home farther down the road.

Marcellus was a farmer who also owned a large apple orchard located on the upper part of their property. Icem said that they had between four hundred and five hundred Pippin, Winesap, and

Icem's father, Marcellus Lawhorne

York apple trees; a man came each season of harvest to buy the fruit, which had been packed in wooden barrels and hauled down the mountain on ground sleds. The barrels were then loaded onto the buyer's truck for reselling. I was surprised to learn that the apples had to be sprayed even back then so that bugs would not infest the fruit.

Icem's original home was located up the mountain from where they now live, and it had the rock outcroppings of Pinnacle Ridge visible in the distance. Icem related that when he was younger, he would climb these rocks to hunt for rattlesnakes. The road up Cox's Creek was only a narrow drag road back then and wasn't paved until much later.

Some of the Lawhornes' neighbors, beside other family members, were the Hendricks, Campbells, and Fitzgeralds. The Hendricks lived higher up from where the original homeplace stood. Icem said that his father later sold the forty acres to the government (US Forest Service) for four dollars an acre but was allowed to continue managing his apple orchard.

Chimney remains of the old Lawhorne homeplace

Icem's mother, Frances, took care of her large family. When I asked what she did during the day, Icem laughed and said, "Cook! She cooked breakfast, and no sooner was that over when she started dinner. When dinner was over, she started in on supper." Peggy added that many times there were extended family members living with them, and the number of people swelled to twelve. The phrase, "A woman's work is never done, from early dawn to setting sun," might have originated in the Lawhorne family. Icem remembers that his mother packed the midday meal for the men working in the orchard and walked up to take their dinner to them.

As with all families blessed with a lot of children, Icem and his brothers and sisters shared in the never-ending work of the self-sufficient mountain lifestyle they were born into. No doubt he did all types of outdoor work, but he seemed drawn to work the land, plowing with horses.

Anyone who knows Icem automatically realizes from his conversation that hunting and fishing have been a top priority throughout his life. His father before him hunted, and as a boy, Icem roamed the mountains and learned to enjoy the challenge of the hunt. He says there are more deer and bear in Virginia now than there were in the earlier years, but as a youngster he was still able to bring some type of game home, and the meat would be consumed by the family. Icem always eats what he kills and does most of the cooking of wild game in his home. At the July pig roasts, people tend to flock to the grill in search of Icem's bear meat before they go for the pork. I know this to be true because I'm usually at the head of the bear meat line!

He attended the early grades at Harmony School, located at the foot of Cox's Creek to the rear of Harmony Presbyterian Church, just as Clemon Lawhorne and Lila Campbell had. He remembers Miss Sanford as the teacher there for many years. The following photograph was taken at Harmony School on May 16, 1925, as the children and some of their parents were enjoying an old-fashioned ice-cream social. Miss Sanford is pictured third from the left in the top row. Many of Icem's family are in the photo, and he is the small blond-headed boy second from right, sitting on the ground next to his brother Daniel.

Ice-cream social at Harmony School (1925)

In later years, he got a job helping to construct the "Skyline" (Blue Ridge Parkway). He said that he was responsible for drilling holes into the rock where explosives were then packed and blasted to clear the way for the coming road. It was hard physical labor, as the drill, which acted much like a jack hammer, pounded its way into solid rock. One hole sixty feet deep would take all day to complete. The following photo was taken in 1941 as construction on the Humpback Rocks campground was underway. Icem is in the middle, looking at the camera.

Constructing Humpback Rocks campground (1941)

The next two photographs were taken in October 1942. The first shows Icem and his little dog, whom he said was a real camera ham, and the second shows Icem (on the left) standing next to his sister Queenetta and cousin Jimmy Lawhorne.

In December of that same year, when Icem was twenty-one years old, he was drafted into the Army/Air Force ground forces. He was shipped to Miami, Florida, for boot camp and just as he was adjusting to the heat, his company was shipped to Salt Lake City, Utah, where he said they about froze to death when they got off the train and stepped into snow about two feet deep.

Icem and friend (October 1942)

He served stateside in California and Kansas but was never shipped overseas during the war because he was in the hospital when his company was sent to Africa. I asked why he was in the hospital, and Icem said that at the time, he had a severely broken wrist. When I inquired how he had broken it, Icem, always a man of few words, replied, "Horseplay!"

He said that while he was in the service, Uncle Sam paid him fifty dollars a month, twenty-five of which he sent back home to his mama. He stayed in the military until 1945 and remembers that the men were out on the airfield when an officer came out and told them the war was over. The officer said that anyone having three or more years of service was to report to headquarters. Icem said that you've never seen so many people stampede across that field!

He came back home to Cox's Creek and took about a month off before

Icem, Queenetta, and Jimmy Lawhorn (October 1942)

Icem in his uniform with his parents

finding employment with a power company that was cutting a right-of-way for power lines being erected along Route 56. I asked if that's when his family got electricity, and both he and Peggy laughed, saying, "No, it went right on by Cox's Creek!" Peggy added that power was not available to the people living on the Creek until the middle 1950s, about the same time the Love community got theirs. Icem later went to work for the Highway Department (then called Public Roads) and retired after thirty-two years on the job.

When Icem was twenty-six years old he married his first wife, Martha, who was the daughter of William and Lillie Lawhorne; after their marriage ceremony at the Lovingston courthouse, the newlyweds came back to live with Icem's parents for a time before moving to the Plumb Campbell home, located up the creek from where his parents lived. The Lawhornes had seven children during their fifteen years of marriage: Ernest, David, Joanne, Ronald, Steve, and two babies who died at birth. Of the remaining five, three survive: Joanne, Ronald, and Steve. Martha passed away when Steve was eight years old, and Icem began raising his youngest son by himself. He built his present home in 1963 and has lived there ever since.

Icem's second wife, Peggy, was born in Amherst County, Virginia, and raised up in Piney River. At eighteen years of age, she joined the Navy and married a career Marine, but later realized that military life could be hard on a family. The couple had three children, but after eighteen years of marriage, Peggy left the union and moved to the Tyro area. Her three boys and Icem's children knew each other from school, so eventually she and Icem met.

Peggy was impressed by the fact that Icem was raising his son by himself, and soon the couple began to date. They married at the Jonesboro Baptist Church parsonage in December 1973, and the marriage that people said wouldn't last is still going strong after thirty-nine years. In addition to their combined children, the Lawhornes currently have eleven grandchildren and seven great-grandchildren in their family.

Anyone acquainted with Icem Lawhorne knows that his name and bear hunting are synonymous. Although the man has hunted most everything there is in the woods, the sport of bear hunting has been at the top of his list ever since he came home from the service in his early twenties. He's kept a line of Redbone and Black-and-Tan dogs to hunt with, saying his best dog was a Redbone by the name of "Jack." Jack was what you'd call a one-man dog, never letting another man come near a downed bear before Icem arrived. Icem has hunted with different men over the years, including members of the Carr, Allen, Evans, Satterwhite, Fitzgerald, Stevens, and Wood families.

The biggest bear he killed weighed 606 pounds and was taken over on Shoe Creek. In my opinion, Icem is one of the last true bear hunters, one who follows his dogs through the rugged mountains on foot without any use of modern-day aids such as tracking collars or GPS devices. He tells stories of bear hunts he's been on that leave you shaking your head in amazement.

Like the one in which he started out on the Big DePriest Mountain and ended up over on Route 60 where the wayside picnic tables are located. I'm not exactly sure how many miles that is, but let's just say it is *way* too far for a normal person to walk. Once he popped out on Route 60, he made his way to a little store and

Bear hunters: Irvin Wood, Henry Carr, Icem, and Elmer Carr

Icem with his 606-pound bear

called Irvin Wood to come pick him up. Irvin asked, "How in the world did you get over here?" Icem told him, "How do you *think* I got over here? I walked!" Of that hunt, Icem said his dogs made

it back home to Cox's Creek about a week later. I bet they wished
they had hitched a ride home, too.

Another incredible story was of the time he was hunting up at
Crabtree with two dogs, and they ran a bear up a tree. Icem was
carrying a single shot shotgun and only wounded the bear, which
fell out of the tree and made for him. One of the dogs was gun
shy and ran off, leaving Icem with no shells in the gun chamber
and only one dog to try to fend off the animal. The bear rushed
at Icem and bit him through the leg, but he managed to get away
and made a run for it.

There was snow and ice on the ground, and they were on a
steep ridge, so Icem grabbed for a bush, but it broke off, sending
him sliding down the side of the mountain. The wounded bear
pursued him, and there was a scary fifteen-minute skirmish during
which the animal continued to lunge at Icem who, in turn, would
kick him away.

In Icem's words, "I finally whupped him, and he ran off and
made for a creek. I found him in the water thrashing around, and
I finished him off." When it was all said and done, some men
came and carried the bear and Icem out together. They took him
to a Doctor Hersley, who had an office in Piney River, who said
he had operated on snake bites and spider bites, but this was the
first bear bite he had ever worked on. The wound was cleaned,
stitched, and left Icem on crutches for a while, but it apparently
never stopped him, as he said he found it awfully hard to squirrel
hunt on crutches!

Another time, one of the dogs ran between his legs, tripping
him. He fell forward, and when he hit the ground, a finger bent
all the way back over his hand, leaving the raw bone sticking out.
Icem sat down on a big oak tree and somehow managed to pull his
finger back in place, piecing the bones back together. He said that
Ral Satterwhite took him to UVA Hospital and when the doctor
looked at it, he said he couldn't have done any better himself. He
also said, "I tell you one thing . . . you're a tough one!"

Bear hunters all have nicknames they go by and they refer to
themselves by these names so often that for years I didn't know a

lot of the men's real names. For instance, Robert Morris's hunting
name is "Apple Picker"; Clifford Stevens is "Polkberry"; Everett
Allen goes by "Bean Head"; and Icem is "Ice Man."

"Ice Man" and "Bean Head" (Icem and Everett Allen)

I asked Icem if, when hunting, he carried a backpack filled
with a lunch, soft drink, or some coffee. He said that he never carried anything extra, only his gun, and many times he didn't wear
a coat! Bear season opens in the month of December, and years
ago our winters were much harsher than they are today, so that
statement amazed me even further. Peggy volunteered that her
husband still works a lot of the time without a coat in the winter
and goes barefoot, to boot. Like I said, the man is tough!

The Lawhornes still maintain a large garden each year, and
so far Peggy hasn't had any luck in trying to get her husband to
downsize. He still cuts firewood to heat their home and keeps busy
doing all types of indoor and outdoor work. He is an excellent
rock mason and has traveled to North Carolina to construct rock
foundations for houses. The Lawhornes have impressive walls
around their home that Icem built from native stone found on
the property. He laughed and said that he might as well make use
of what they have the most of.

The stone wall that Icem constructed

Taking a break from his rock work

The Lawhornes are still active at Harmony Presbyterian Church at the foot of Cox's Creek, and Peggy preaches there on the first and third Sundays of each month. She started out as a church elder, and the congregation encouraged her to take some classes on church policy and record keeping. She continued to take different classes over the course of three years, and it was at this point that their pastor quit. The congregation asked Peggy to fill the vacancy. She has been at it ever since and shares the pulpit with Bill Aikens who covers the Sundays Peggy doesn't preach. Peggy is humble about her call to the ministry and says that she depends on God to give her the words the people need to encourage them in their faith.

Icem continues to fish regularly on local lakes and rivers, mostly for bass, but in the past he loved to fish for native trout

A full rack of turkey beards

also. He still likes to turkey hunt and tells of the time he was sitting in a blind one morning and had already killed and cleaned a bird and was calling in another, when a huge bobcat sailed right into the blind, almost knocking him over and stringing the blind down the hill.

Icem remarked that the cat probably heard the gobble of the turkey caller and smelled the fresh meat and decided to make a raid. The next fall, Icem set a steel trap, and he caught a bobcat weighing thirty-six pounds, which is a big cat. Icem has a building that is filled with all types of trophies, and it's kind of a hangout during hunting season. Peggy's dry humor made us laugh as she said, "It's hard to maintain a high class, sophisticated life with Icem."

Icem with a few of his deer racks (1998)

The Lawhornes enjoy bluegrass music and can be seen dancing at the various places where the music is played on a regular basis. Peggy likes to play music on her autoharp and Dobro and always plays when they have their annual pig picnic, held on the last Saturday in July. She also grows beautiful flowers; the grounds around their home are meticulously kept, and they share a covered bridge at the entrance to their property with Clemon Lawhorne.

Icem showing a large, 12-point buck rack

Covered bridge to the Lawhornes' house

The grounds at Icem and Peggy's

As the interview came to a close, the camera came out, and we took a few pictures before heading back up the mountain toward home. My favorite was the one I took of Icem and Peggy, still looking happy and content after all these years of marriage. Billy

Icem and Peggy at their Cox's Creek home

and I enjoyed the warm conversation and the welcoming spirit we felt at the Lawhorne home, and we thank them again for letting us come to record their oral histories and make them a part of *Appalachian Heart*.

LaRue Fauber Wilson

14

LaRue Fauber Wilson

Although I've known LaRue casually down through the years, I'd never had the pleasure of sitting down with her one on one and finding out about her early upbringing and what her interests have been as an adult. All I can say is that it has been my loss. LaRue is truly an amazing woman who can do anything she sets her mind to, and that, my friends, is quite a lot!

Along with many other talents, music has been first on her list all through her life. It seems that whenever I was at a function where LaRue was, she had a guitar strapped around her neck and was standing in a circle, jamming with other musicians. She is the only woman I've met who reminded me most of my best friend Gladys Coffey, who was another person who could do nearly everything there was to do.

The evening I rode out to LaRue's farm for the interview, I knew there would be no possible way to do justice to the wealth of talent this woman possesses. This chapter is only the tip of the iceberg, but I hope it will somewhat capture the essence of who LaRue Wilson really is.

LaRue's father was Hercy Franklin Fauber, the son of David Fauber and Celina Fauber; her mother was Lottie Virginia Campbell Fauber, daughter of Howard Donald "Pet" Campbell and Elena Coffey Campbell, whose family started out living on Irish Creek but later moved to Roanoke and spent the rest of their lives

LaRue's maternal great-grandfather,
John Coffey

LaRue's maternal great-grandmother,
Patra Tyler Coffey

there. Going back one generation further, LaRue's great-grandparents on her mother's side were John and Patra Tyler Coffey.

Born on April 16, 1929, LaRue was the fifth and last child in the family; her siblings before her were Novella, Harry, Myrtle, and Agnes. The five Fauber children were all raised in the same mountain homeplace as their father, Hercy, and their farm was one of the most beautiful pieces of property in our area.

LaRue's parents, Hercy and Lottie Fauber

The Fauber homeplace on the Blue Ridge Parkway in later years

The farm sat high on a flat ridge and had grassy fields sloping downward to Dowell's Ridge below it. The nearly four hundred acres was used to pasture cows, horses, hogs, and sheep, and was a beautiful setting for their pristine home, barn, outbuildings, and gardens. LaRue said that the large flock of sheep that her daddy kept were sold and sheared for their wool; spring lambs were sometimes butchered for meat.

The sheep that Hercy Fauber kept

The Faubers kept a line of fine riding horses that were some-times sold or used for racing purposes. When asked if they were thoroughbreds, LaRue said that she didn't think so; they were just nice horses, healthy and shiny and could run like the wind. LaRue said that her father and her brother Harry entered the horses in races around the area and won a lot of the time. Her mother loved to ride also and had a horse named Louise that would stand calmly for her to mount, but once she was in the saddle, the spirited horse was known to take off.

Hercy Fauber on one of his horses

One time, her mother had been out picking blackberries and was riding Louise home with the bucket of berries slung over her arm. They got to the fence, and her mother was in the process of dismounting to open the gate, when Louise jumped clear over top of it, her mother hanging on for dear life. She never fell off, but LaRue laughed and said Louise was like that, "She didn't want to stand around!"

When the construction of the Blue Ridge Parkway began, the government sliced off abound ninety acres from the front of the home to be used for the road and as buffer between the house and the scenic highway. Later, the property was sold to a wealthy businessman and was commonly known from that time as the "Skylark Farm." In chapter 3, Lowell Humphreys goes into more detail about Skylark, since he and his wife, Viola, were the caretakers of the large farm for thirty-nine years.

LaRue's mother, Lottie, at the family farm

LaRue said that to some, it may not have looked as if they had a lot of material goods, but in her eyes, they had everything they needed for a life of plenty: a nice farm, food to eat, and good health to enjoy it all. Their closest neighbors were about a mile away and included members of the Bradley, Robinson, and Falls families. She worked around the farm doing everything from housework to garden chores, and she also loved to work in the fields when her father was making hay. She said that they didn't have a tractor back then but had these big hay forks mounted on top of the barn; the forks would grab the loose hay off the wagon, then the hay would be lifted to the top of the haymow by horses that were hooked to a pulley. It was LaRue's job—so her brother, Harry, had decided—to be in the haymow to spread out the loose hay when it was dropped.

In the hot summertime, LaRue said that she would just about smother in the confined space where she couldn't get a breath of fresh air, and Harry would delight in dropping the large load of hay on top of her head. She laughed and said it's a wonder she has any sense at all. She helped with shearing the sheep by turning the handle on the shearing clippers, which her father said she turned smoother than anyone else. They had fruit trees and vegetables from the garden that were either canned or put inside the ground house where they would keep cool.

Like many of the young children who lived in this area, LaRue attended the Mill Creek School, walking a path through the mountains for about three miles to get to school. Mill Creek had one room with classes from the first to the seventh grades.

Mill Creek schoolhouse

When snow was on the ground, LaRue said that Harry, who was a good bit older, would scrape the road for them. She remembers one time he didn't, and she and some friends got stuck in a snowdrift and played around and laughed until it was too late to go to school, so they came back home. LaRue said that one of the teachers she liked a lot boarded with her family during that particular school year, which was a common practice at that time.

One of her favorite school chums was George Allen, with whom she loved to go rabbit hunting. I asked if they had dogs and was told, "No, it was just us, chasing through the mountains. I come in late one day from school, and Father met me at the gate, asking, 'Where have you been little daughter?' 'Me and George were tracking rabbits.' He said, 'Your mother has about worried herself to death wondering where you were.' I said, 'Well good lands, what time is it?' And it was about six thirty in the evening." I inquired as to whether or not she got a whipping, and LaRue said she never got a whipping in her life, but her dad thumped her on the head with his thumb, and they had a good laugh over it.

Although her family did not play any type of musical instrument, her father had a beautiful voice and sang in the choir at Mount Paran Baptist Church, where the family attended. But at an early age, LaRue found that she was completely captivated by string music and asked for a guitar when she was around ten years old. Her parents bought her a good Gibson, and she's been at it ever since.

I asked how she became interested in playing, since none of her family had any influence on her in that direction. Her answer of "I grew up with the Allens" needed no explanation; in this area, members of the Allen family were renowned for having some of the top musical talent in Virginia. LaRue remembers going home with George and his sister Irene, and they would play music with George's daddy, Pug Allen, until

LaRue at age ten with her first guitar

the wee hours of the morning. Pug would call and tell her to be ready in a half an hour, and he would be by to pick her up to go play somewhere.

LaRue learned to play the fiddle next, and she can play the Dobro, mandolin, and banjo as well. To this day, she cannot read music but says emphatically that playing by ear is the *only* way to play.

LaRue as a teenager with some cousins

She was in her early twenties, playing with a group at a dance held at the Brownsburg School, when she met James Moore Wilson, Jr., whom she described as very handsome and sophisticated with a pipe in his mouth. The Wilson family lived in Raphine, just across the road from the farm where LaRue presently lives. Jim was a student at Virginia Tech; when his father became ill, he came home from college to help on the farm.

His mother was a teacher for thirty-five years at the Virginia School for the Deaf and Blind in Staunton. LaRue said that Jim took her home in his convertible that night after the dance, and they began to date regularly. The couple courted for about a year before marrying on April 11, 1952, at New Providence Presbyterian Church; Dr. Locke White officiated the service.

The newlyweds honeymooned in Nashville, Tennessee, staying at the Gaylord Hotel and celebrating by going to the Ryman Auditorium to watch the Grand Ole Opry. For their twenty-fifth anniversary, their children surprised them with a week's stay in Nashville, back at the Gaylord Hotel and Grand Ole Opry where

they'd begun life as a married couple. When the Wilsons returned from their honeymoon, they lived in the Ladd area, where Jim was employed as a farm manager for the Quillen family, who owned the Waynesboro Nurseries. They lived there about three and a half years before buying and moving to a large farm in Raphine, across the road from where Jim had been raised and where LaRue continues to live.

The stately home was built in the early 1800s and has lovely large rooms with the

LaRue and Jim Wilson on their wedding day (April 11, 1952)

high ceilings of the time. The farm also came with an array of barns and log outbuildings that only added to the beauty of the property. The Wilsons raised cattle and sheep on the farm, and Jim was also employed at the Westinghouse Company in Verona; he retired after thirty-five years of service.

The Wilson's had eight children: Glenn, Faith, Mike, Denise,

The Wilson farm

Linda, Jerry, and twin daughters, Lisa and Laura, whom LaRue said were a real surprise, even for Dr. Davis, who delivered all her babies at Waynesboro Community Hospital. LaRue was fortunate enough to be able to stay home to raise their children and not leave their upbringing to someone else.

Jim and LaRue's family

LaRue jamming with friends

While her husband worked a public job, LaRue was a true farm wife, taking care of the livestock, including delivering spring lambs and calves. She and Jim had a good life, doing things together that they both enjoyed. Although he could play the fiddle, LaRue said that her husband was shy about playing with a group and was content to just go along and listen whenever she would play.

LaRue playing Dobro with "Possum's Delight"

LaRue said that over the years she has played country, old time ballads, and bluegrass with a lot of different people on a lot of different instruments in a lot of different places. She was a long-time member of Bill Mason's group, "Possum's Delight," and was with him for fifteen years. She was also a regular Friday night band member at Clark's Old Time Music Center in Raphine for nine years. She has traveled to Buena Vista, Roanoke, Floyd, and Galax—and places in between—just to play music. She still goes to Manley Allen's from time to time, and Jerry Allen is now pestering her to come over to Rockfish Valley to join in the fun on Thursday nights at the Rockfish Fire Department. She laughed and said that since Jerry is a state trooper, maybe she'd better listen to him and go to try it out when the weather breaks.

As I said before, LaRue is a woman of many talents, and I laughed when she told me the story of how she had shown Jim a new pair of shoes she'd bought, and he said they were the worst-looking things he'd ever seen. His petite wife then told him they were clogging shoes and that she had signed up to take clogging lessons. Jim's only comment was to say, "Oh, for pity's sake!" She went on with her plans and got a certificate and danced for a while with the Shenandoah Cloggers. She said it is great exercise, and when she told her doctor what she was doing, he about died laughing.

Jim passed away on January 17, 2008, and LaRue has continued to stay on the farm with the help of her children, who now take care of a lot of the work. She continues to love to work both inside and outside the home and is busy living life, going places when she wants to. In fact, when setting up a time for this interview, LaRue said it would have to be in the evening, since she does so many things during the daytime hours.

And the things she does! She has worked on the rock foundations for some of the old log outbuildings, as well as rechinking the cement in between the logs. She showed me a downstairs bathroom that she had tiled all by herself, and the rooms in the home are beautifully stenciled by her own hand. She says she loves to paint the walls, and she does artistic painting as well.

She still helps her sons with the outside mowing, and by her own admission, she likes to keep on the go continually and feels it's good for a person to keep busy and active.

The walls of the home are covered with LaRue's handwork, including framed pictures of intricate cross-stitch and crewel work she has done over the years. Each piece is a treasure and destined to become Wilson family heirlooms in the future. She sews and when asked what it is she makes, LaRue said, "Anything I want to." Up the stairs we went for a tour of her sewing room, and when the door opened and the light was switched on, I realized the magnitude of her hobby.

LaRue's sewing room

There were three different sewing machines in the room, including an old Montgomery Ward console she got when she married. There were tubs and tubs full of the most beautiful material I had ever laid eyes on. One closet was filled from floor to ceiling with more material, and I had to chuckle at a sign hanging on the back of the closet door that said it all. LaRue said that she has so much material, if she sewed pieces together and quilted them, she could cover the whole state of Virginia!

A closetful of quilt material

Of all the beautiful things she makes, my personal favorite has to be the wealth of handmade quilts and quilt hangings she stitches together. Patterns include bow tie, crazy quilt, log cabin, flower basket, drunkard's path, attic window, and many original creations, such as mountain, pond, and flower scenes that LaRue has designed herself. What strikes one most is the blending of the colors, which she certainly has an eye for.

Besides hand quilting, she also quilts by machine in a style called "free motion," which has no set sewing pattern but is a free-

A humorous sign in LaRue's sewing room

hand type of stitch that leaves each quilt block different. She also names and dates each of her quilts with a handwritten patch on the underside, so people years from now will know who made each piece and when. After a solid hour looking at different quilts, the night was wearing on, and I told LaRue that I had better get back up the mountain. Her response really made me laugh. "You haven't

LaRue working on a quilt

even seen the best quilts yet!" I know I'll have to make a return trip so she can bring them out and show them off.

As we went downstairs and I prepared to leave, LaRue switched on the outside light; she walked out with me and said she couldn't wait for spring to come so that she could get started on her project of rechinking one of the log outbuildings. Climbing into my car I had to smile and marvel again at all the talent wrapped up in one tiny package called LaRue Fauber Wilson.

Vera Falls (Spy Run Gap)

William Henry Coffey

15

William Henry Coffey

I'm not exactly sure when or where I first met William. His family is so large and extended that no doubt he was somewhere around when I was covering a story for the *Backroads* newspaper about one of his relatives. He had nine sisters, so there were plenty of opportunities to be at reunions, church functions, birthdays, anniversaries, and general get-togethers. The one thing that stood out whenever I saw William was the signature way in which he wore his hat: cocked off to one side of his head.

He was a lifelong logger by trade, and I interviewed him and his partner of twenty-nine years, Sonny Taylor, for the November 2006 logging issue of *Backroads*. Billy and I were privileged to be invited over to Don Taylor's camp in White Rock where he and William were spending a week during hunting season. Don wanted us to come for a meal, which William cooked, and we never forgot the company or the delicious food that was served up. Brown beans with fatback, fried cabbage, potatoes, pork tenderloin, and cornbread made the old mountain way in a cast-iron skillet—poured thin in the skillet and baked until crispy. Billy talked about that cornbread for days, until I finally called William and asked for his recipe—which I still use today.

In the three previous Backroads books, I wasn't able to put everyone I wanted to in each volume, so when it was decided that *Appalachian Heart* would be published, William was on my "to do" list. Luckily for me and for you readers, he said yes when asked about the interview. I spent a wonderful morning at his and wife Kitty's home, asking questions about his growing up years along the North

Fork of the Tye River; then they graciously posed for photographs for this book. Somehow it wouldn't have been complete without his life story, and I feel blessed to know the rugged mountain man who is loved and respected by family and friends alike.

William's grandparents on his father's side were William Henry Coffey, for whom William was named, and Nannie Dinsmore Coffey. On his mother's side were Wilda Sorrells and Ida Fitzgerald Sorrells. William's parents were Clarence Henry Coffey and Maywood Sorrells

William's father, Clarence Coffey

Coffey. All his people came from the North Fork of the Tye River area, and that's where William and his sisters were raised up.

William's mother (right) as a child with her sister, Lovie

William's siblings, in the order of their births, were: Alice and Harry, who both died shortly after birth; eight girls, Vivian, Velma, Vera, Elaine, Genevieve, Georgie, Betty, and Shirley; and on April 25, 1942, William, the last child born to his parents, came into the world. William was born at his aunt Lovie's home, which was located up above Durham's Run on the North Fork Road that parallels the Tye River. When he was about eighteen months old, Clarence and Maywood separated, and the family moved quite a few times but always stayed along the North Fork. William lived mostly with his father, but he was basically raised by his older sisters.

When he was seven years of age, they moved to a home built on the side of the road closer to Durham's Run. It was at this time that his father had a store, a mill, and a sawmill on the property close to the house; William, as well as all his sisters, worked in the

Young William with sisters, Georgie, Elaine, and Betty

sawmill. The store was built over a little creek running down out of the mountains, and the water flowed right under the building. William was a child then, but he still remembers people coming in to buy coffee, paying for it with paper stamps that came inside coffee cans and was used as currency.

When William was around nine, they moved to a fifty-two-acre farm that belonged to Saylor Allen and was high on the mountain to the right of Durham's Run. Clarence then bought more acreage from Roy Allen that adjoined the property, which went all the way down to White Rock. Although the property is now forest, back then William said that the land was cleared and corn was planted.

There was a house, a big barn to keep the livestock in, and an orchard. He remembers his daddy inviting a bunch of people to come over on Saturdays and Sundays to pick blackberries by the washtubful. The berries were eaten fresh, made into jelly, or canned for future use. There were two graveyards on the property, and a child of Saylor Allen's was buried in the orchard on the fifty-two acres; there was another cemetery high on a ridge on the Roy Allen property.

The old White Rock School was closed by the time William was six years old, so he and his sister Shirley had to walk several miles down the mountain to Hercy Coffey's store where they caught the bus to Fleetwood Elementary School in Massies Mill. William remembers that some of his bus drivers were Parrish Strickland, Bob Loving, Wilson Lawhorne, and Harold Campbell.

William's school photo
at six years of age

When William and Shirley got off the school bus in the afternoon, they walked back to Durham's Run, up the steep, rocky road to what they called Pleas's mountain, where the family's seven cows were grazed, then brought the cows down by Raymond Allen's camp, across the creek, put them on the path that ran through the mountains between the two houses, then drove them home. Once home, they had to milk them all and bring in wood for the heating and cooking stoves. After the cows were milked, the children would take gallon crocks and strain the fresh milk into them, put the crocks in the springhouse, and place a clean plate on top of each with a rock to hold it down, so that the crock would not float up out of the water.

William said he'd grab a piece of cornbread and head to the

springhouse to eat cornbread with the thick buttermilk. The children did this day after day, in all kinds of weather. William was eight years old at the time, Shirley, ten. After supper, he helped with the dishes before he could start his homework. Because he was raised with so many sisters, William learned to do all kinds of housework and cooking, which has served him well throughout his life.

William with seven of his nine sisters

William loves to hunt, and he was just a young boy when he first headed to the woods to hunt squirrels with a .22 rifle or a shotgun. He remembers that when he was about nine years old, his brother-in-law Delbert Phillips was walking down the road with a single-barreled shotgun; William had always wanted to shoot the gun, but Delbert said he'd have to ask his daddy for permission.

Delbert said, "Clarence, this boy wants to shoot this gun."

Clarence replied, "Well, let him shoot it!"

I asked William if the "kick" of the gun made him fall down, and he said it was worse than that. Delbert loaded the gun with a .00

buckshot shell but didn't tell William to hold it tight against his shoulder when he pulled the trigger so that the impact wouldn't hurt him. William said, "When that thing went off, it ripped me from my shoulder down to my belt and laid my belly open. I never let on that it hurt me a bit, but I was sore for weeks afterward. I was afraid if I told them it hurt me, they wouldn't let me shoot it no more!"

William has hunted ever since, preferring deer and squirrels, but he's killed two bear also. When he was in his teens working with Carl and Ralph Coffey, he said that they had an old double-barreled shotgun. He wanted to go squirrel hunting, and they told him to take that gun so he wouldn't have to reload every time he shot. William went to the woods and was sitting on a big rock when he saw a squirrel coming down the side of a tree. He said both triggers were placed close together and when he pulled the gun up to shoot, he mistakenly hit both. When they went off, William laughed out loud and said, "It liked to stomp me!" When I asked if there was anything left of the squirrel, we laughed even harder as he admitted, "I completely missed it!"

William's mother lived with different relatives after she and Clarence were separated, and William didn't see much of her during his growing up years. His father had a girlfriend named Carrie Fitzgerald who moved in while they were living on the Saylor Allen farm, and she already had a young son named Lester, who came with her. Two children were born from Clarence and Carrie's union: a boy by the name of J. D. and a daughter, Josephine.

William's father was working in Maryland when he had an accident and was hit in the head with a pipe. He never was the same after that, and he began having mental problems. In September 1955, he was admitted to Western State Hospital in Staunton, where he spent the next twenty-five years, passing away in 1980 at eighty-one years of age. William's mother had died six years earlier in 1974.

When his father was hospitalized, William began living first with one sister, then another, but each lived farther away, making it harder for him to catch the bus to school. So at age thirteen, he quit school and went to work. There was a man by the name of Martin Luther Fitzgerald, who had bought some logs from Clarence before he was hospitalized, and young William skidded the logs out with Mr. Fitzgerald's horse, which William was allowed to keep at the homeplace until the work was done. He was paid forty cents an hour and thought he was making good money earning $3.20 a day.

After he finished the work for Mr. Fitzgerald, he stayed with Quincey Coffey and began logging with her two sons, Carl and Ralph. The boys cut timber with crosscut saws and skidded logs out of the woods with an ox named "Mike." William also helped Fred Zirkle log for a time, staying with Lena Zirkle and others up and down the North Fork.

Thus began William's lifetime career of logging, which he continues to love. When asked what he likes best about his chosen work, he says being his own boss and working in the outdoors. Or, as William puts it, "It gets in your blood, and you can't quit!"

He loved cutting the actual trees, but at seventy-one years of age, arthritis has forced him to hire his nephew Jerry Bryant to do the cutting now. Jerry's brother, Larry, has also helped William drive the logging truck whenever needed. Jerry's young son, Joseph, who no doubt will be part of the next generation of loggers, drives the truck and skidder on weekends when he's out of school. William says Joseph watches him "like a hawk watching a chicken," and whatever he asks the boy to do, he never hesitates to do it.

When William was nineteen years old, he went to a dance held in Verona with his cousin Dale Allen and met his future wife, Kitty. She was sitting by the side of the building with her sister and a bunch of other girls when Kitty whispered, "I would love to dance with that guy over there wearing the yellow shirt." To her supreme embarrassment, her sister walked up to William and told him what she had said. He took the hint and promptly walked over to ask for the next dance. The rest, as they say, is history. After that night, William bought his first car, courted Kitty for four years, and they married on January 22, 1965.

Kitty, whose given name is Virginia Katherine, was born on December 25, 1942 to parents Lloyd and Ressie Bodkin of Highland County, Virginia. She had nine siblings, six brothers and three sisters, and was two years old when the family moved to a farm in Mount Crawford.

The newlyweds started housekeeping in Mount Crawford, then moved in with William's sister Velma who lived along Back Creek at the foot of Love Mountain. From there they came out to the Stuarts Draft area and lived for a time with Earl Coffey. William heard that a house was for sale down the road from Earl, so he went to look at the place; he and Kitty said that it needed a lot of work.

They contacted the owner, Lewis Martin, who lived in Rockfish, and found out that he wanted to sell the house, not just rent it. As they talked, it came out that William's daddy and Lewis had dealt in cattle together in the past, so the man warmed up to the couple and offered to sell the house to them for five thousand dollars. William told him his asking price was too steep for his budget, so Mr. Martin said, "I'll tell you what I'll do. If you gather up five hundred dollars and bring it over to me, I will finance the house and sell it to you for forty-eight hundred dollars."

William explained that it might be a little while before he could get the money and was told, "It will be there." After William brought Mr. Martin the money, they moved in and found they could afford the $60.60 monthly payments! The home was set on a double lot that was about an acre of land known as the "Rivermont" lot. Kitty said there were only a few houses around them at that time; the surrounding property was mostly farmland, which suited the young couple because they wanted to be off by themselves.

Over the years, the Coffeys made many improvements, such as modernizing the kitchen, adding a porch, and having the outside bricked. They continue to reside there after forty-eight years of marriage.

William and his half-brother, J. D. Fitzgerald, were cutting pulpwood when he and Kitty married, and William logged with a few other people before buying his first logging truck in 1967 from the Blue Ridge Grocery in Waynesboro. He laughed as he told me it was a 1961 Ford with the letters IGA printed on the side! With the purchase of his own truck, Coffey Logging Company was in business.

Their first son, Billy, was born on July 13, 1968, right after they moved in to their new house; the youngest, David, came into the world on December 29, 1970. Although the boys are not loggers by trade like their daddy, both grew up around it

William, Kitty, and their two sons, Billy (far right) and David

and help whenever needed. Kitty bragged on the boys by saying they were always good kids and never got into the trouble that many of the other teenagers of that time did.

Other than having a few different jobs during his lifetime, William Henry has been and continues to be in the logging profession. He's worked with different men over the years: Don Taylor, Everett Allen, Dennis Allen, and nephews Marvin Phillips, Jerry Bryant, and Dale Allen. Dennis was William's uncle, and William

William when he began logging with Sonny Taylor

remembers staying with him to cut extract wood on the mountain at Wintergreen. The extract, which was standing dead chestnut wood, was taken to a mill in Buena Vista, where it was processed into dyes.

William and Kitty when she helped log

In 1971, William went into a partnership with Sonny Taylor that lasted for twenty-nine years before Sonny retired. When Sonny wasn't available to log, Kitty went to the woods and helped her husband by driving the skidder and sometimes the logging truck.

The two men grew up together along the North Fork of the Tye River in Nelson County and have made a lot of memories together working side by side in the woods. They both learned the logging trade from family members and friends who were in the business.

William with his longtime partner, Sonny Taylor, and nephew, Marvin Phillips

A healthy load of logs

The men each had trucks and began accumulating all kinds of equipment, starting with an Allis Chalmers crawler with a front-end loader, so they wouldn't have to roll the cut logs on the truck with cant hooks any longer. They invested in some McCulloch saws and a flatbed trailer; William remembers that their first job was in White Hall, where they cut several hundred thousand feet of lumber that was then hauled to the Ramsey sawmill in Shipman and Yancey Mills near Crozet. They didn't do any clear-cutting and stuck to select cutting, which took the larger timber.

William loading logs on the knuckle boom

William's Fourth of July parade "float"

As time went on, they invested in better equipment, including a 440 John Deere skidder that they used for eighteen months before trading up to a new 1975 Franklin skidder. When I had asked Sonny if it had more power, he said, "It was ready to go when I wasn't!" Old saws were replaced by large Stihl saws and a newer Mack truck.

William drove his big, red Mack truck for many years, and one time he entered it fully loaded with logs into the Fourth of July parade in Stuarts Draft. He laughed when he told me that before he got to the end of the parade, someone had bought the entire load of logs from him.

When asked what the most difficult jobs were that they'd tackled, William said there was one on Cub Creek and another on Jack's Hill that were particularly steep and dangerous. Neither William nor Sonny were ever seriously hurt while logging; like most of the men in the business, they've toppled some equipment but escaped without too much damage to themselves.

When they first started out, the men went around asking people if they wanted the timber cut off their land. But in later years, people began calling them because of their reputation for being fair and honest men.

The largest tree they ever harvested was located in Batesville. When it hit the ground, they discovered that it was a bee tree, loaded with honey in the top. That particular tree ended up having five thousand board feet in it and was so large that Yancey Mills did not have the equipment to saw it; a man by the name of Charles Trussel of Lexington bought it for veneer.

Another big tree located in Fishersville was blown down by a storm before William cut it. It was a white oak that had close to three thousand board feet in it when he took it to Calvert Fitzgerald's sawmill in Fairfield, where he sells most of his logs. It was so large that William looks dwarfed in the photos taken at the site while loading it with his knuckle boom and when he and his son Billy had it loaded on the truck.

All through the years, William and Sonny Taylor remained friends; when Sonny passed away in December 2011, it left an

William dwarfed by a huge fallen tree in Fishersville

Loading the enormous white oak tree in Fishersville

empty spot in William's heart, along with the hearts of many others who knew and loved him.

Other friends and loggers kid William and call him all sorts of funny names, such as "John H.," "Wee Willie," and currently the "Grape Ape," after the dark-blue Mack truck he now drives.

William and son Billy with the Fishersville tree

William and Kitty continue to be active and do whatever they want. Kitty has worked for the last fifteen years driving the bus for the handicapped, taking students to the Wilson elementary and high schools. Their son Billy and his wife, Tara, have three boys and one girl. David is going with a sweet girl from Stuarts Draft, Lindsay Lowery. Of William's nine sisters, three survive—Josephine Carr of Stuarts Draft, Georgie Phillips and Vera Falls, both of Vesuvius—and he is close to all three, as well as his nieces, nephews, cousins, and grandchildren.

William with his three surviving sisters: Josephine, Georgie, and Vera (April 2012)

As the interview came to a close, I asked William what the best part of his life has been. Kitty chimed in by saying, "It was when he got married!" We all had a good laugh, then William said that next to that, he loved his work as a logger.

William Henry Coffey is a gentle giant with a kind heart who clearly loves his family. Even with all the hard knocks he had during his formative years, I told him that he's turned out pretty well. He smiled, cocked his ball cap, and replied, "Well, I think so! Not to have any education or a whole lot of opportunities in life, I think I've done pretty well, too."

William and Kitty at their Stuarts Draft home

Ruby Nannie Coffey

16

Ruby Nannie Coffey

I met Ruby and her family shortly after moving to Love, Virginia, in the summer of 1980. Ruby's father was the brother of my up-the-road neighbor and good friend, Johnny Coffey, who was featured in the first Backroads book, *Plain Folk and Simple Livin'*.

Ruby lived with her parents, Forest and Eva, in a home in the Love community they had built and moved to in 1961. Up to that time, they had lived over in the holler on the east side of the Blue Ridge Parkway where my husband Billy's family was from. Today that same area is known as Chicken Holler, but Ruby said that when she was growing up, the older people just called it the holler, and that's how she has always referred to it.

I remember two incidents after moving here, both involving Ruby, that endeared her to me for the more than thirty years I have known her. The first was when we came to visit one evening, and I went to leave by the front door. We had entered through the back door, and when I reached for the front doorknob, Ruby yanked my hand off it, made an "X" mark on the floor with her foot, and said that it was bad luck not to leave the same way you came in. The "X," I was told, cancelled out the error on my part, thus eliminating the bad luck. This was my first introduction to the superstitions that have been a big part of the mountain people's lives down through the generations.

The second incident was on Halloween as I was driving my daughter up and down the mountain for trick-or-treating. When we headed away from the suburban neighborhood with houses packed right next to each other, Heather was worried she'd get shortchanged on candy because there weren't as many people farther out. Turns out, there weren't as many children here on the mountain either, so in the end, folks tended to be very generous with their giving. Having lived in the city, I had cautioned Heather about taking apples from people because of the scary reports of razor blades inserted in them.

On this particular Halloween night, I pulled into Ruby's driveway and sat in the car while Heather went to the door. When Ruby handed her a large red apple, she glanced at it, then back at me, with a questioning look in her eye. I yelled, "Don't take it; it's probably got a razor blade in it!" Ruby calmly assured her the apple was safe, and Heather, satisfied, was on her way back to the car when Ruby called her back. She handed Heather another apple and told her, "Here, give this one to your mother . . . it *has* a razor blade in it!" I laughed and laughed and never forgot her humor.

We attended church together, as well as homecomings, parties, and funerals. Ruby lived at home and took care of her parents for as long as they lived. She's been a big part of my life here in Love, Virginia, and always will be. For that reason, I am honored to write her life story in this final chapter of *Appalachian Heart* as a testament to the kindness and resiliency of the mountain people.

Ruby's grandparents on her mother's side were Ailet Campbell and his wife, Arminta, who lived in and around the Love area and later in Fishersville. Her paternal grandparents were Tom Coffey and his wife, Nannie, who made their home in the same holler where Ruby was raised. Ruby remembers both sets of grandparents well and how they walked back and forth to visit frequently. The Campbell side of the family was laid to rest in the Mountain View Mennonite Church Cemetery at the bottom of the mountain. Ailet died in 1959, Arminta (who was called "Mint") in 1962. The Coffey grandparents, great-grandparents, a twin brother and sister of Ruby's, as well as other ancestors were buried in the Coffey family cemetery located on their property in the holler.

Ruby was eleven years old when her grandmother, Nannie Coffey, died in August 1935. "It was near my birthday, and we took the horses and went to Hercy Coffey's Store on Tye River where [Nannie] bought enough material to make me a dress. We

Ruby's grandparents, Ailet and Arminta Campbell (top); her mother, Eva; and Eva's two brothers, Odie and Woodrow

came back to our house, and my grandparents spent the night with us. She started to get sick right after supper, and she died the next day. The doctor said she died of acute indigestion."

Ruby also remembers the funeral of her grandfather Coffey, the last person to be buried back at the homeplace. Tom died on January 19, 1955, and Ruby said that on the day of the funeral it was so cold and snowy that after the service, which was held at Mountain Top Christian Church, they weren't sure that the hearse would be able to pull the steep grade back to the cemetery, so Tom's coffin was put in the back of a four-wheel-drive truck to get there.

Several tragic stories originated from the holler. One was the death of Henry Campbell, who was helping Tom Coffey burn a large brush pile. He had volunteered to stay with the fire while the rest of the men went back to the house to eat dinner. Upon returning, the men were horrified to find that Henry had somehow fallen into the fire and burned up. The only things that were left were his shoes.

Another tale was told to me by Ruby's uncle, Johnny Coffey. He said they had all gone to the night meeting (revival) at Mountain Top Church, and when the service was over, they noticed an orange glow in the night sky from down in the holler. Johnny said they all ran for home and found his father's house engulfed in flames. Everything was lost, and from that time on, Tom lived with various family members, spending most of his time with a nephew, Ellis Coffey, who lived in Staunton.

Ruby's parents met during the time her mother's family was living in the village of Love. Most people attended Mountain Top Christian Church at the top of the mountain, and many a match was forged at those early services. Eva Campbell was fifteen years of age when she married Forest Coffey, who was two years older at seventeen. At this point in her narration, Ruby laughed, shook her head, and commented on their young age; she wondered why their parents had let them marry so early. But that seemed to be the custom in the mountains, and I've heard people say that a woman of twenty who wasn't married was considered an old maid.

The young couple lived with Forest's parents, Tom and Nannie, for several years and their first child, Houston, was born there in 1918. Forest's brother, Johnny, and his wife, Nin, also lived there, and their two sons, Malcolm and Winfred, were also born in that house. Ruby said that she had a brother and sister (twins) born on April 9, 1922, but the boy is thought to have been still-born and the girl, whom they named Pauline, died a few days later on April 14, 1922. They were buried in the family grave-yard. Ruby said that one time, her mother showed her some little clothes she had made for the twins before their birth that she kept inside a shoebox.

Eventually Forest and Eva bought a two-story home from Forest's uncle, Peter Coffey, that was just a short distance from Tom and Nannie's place. Downstairs, the home had a kitchen and two bedrooms that were often used as sitting rooms. There was a stairway leading upstairs to a wide hall that had bedrooms on either side.

The old homeplace in the holler

Ruby was the first child to be born in the new home and came into the world on August 13, 1924. Her parents gave her two middle names, Nannie and Arminta, after her two grandmothers, but she has always used Nannie as her official middle name.

Her brother Richard was born in 1928, and sisters Madeline in 1932 and Louise in 1936. Of the five children, only three still survive: Ruby, Richard, and Madeline.

When asked what life was like when she was growing up, Ruby said that they all worked in the corn field located on a hill up behind the house, and she remembers that the oldest child would always help take care of infant children, who were put in a little box in the shade.

At noontime, Eva would walk back to the house to prepare a large dinner for the working family. After the meal was eaten, the family went back to hoe corn until suppertime. Ruby said that her dad, like all the people living in the holler, worked the land with horses. The Coffeys also kept cows, which were milked, and the milk was then put in a springhouse that had a trough of water running through it to keep the milk cold. Butter was made from the cream, and it, too, was kept fresh and cool in the springhouse.

Ruby remarked that she and her sister Madeline would walk to a lower orchard to get the cows, and they were never afraid, even though the mountains were much wilder back then. Some of the cows wore leather collars with bells attached to them so that they could be located more easily when it was time to drive them home. The family kept a flock of chickens for household use, and Forest also raised chickens for the Weaver Hatchery in Stuarts Draft that supplied all the feed. The eggs were eaten as well as traded along with butter at country stores for staples such as coffee, sugar, and salt—anything the family could not raise or grow at home.

Eva canned vegetables as well as meat, and Ruby remembers that they also buried potatoes, turnips, and cabbages. A hole was dug in the ground and lined with leaves or straw, and the vegetables would be put inside and covered up with dirt. The food would keep all winter long, and all you had to do was dig them out when needed.

Like every other person who lived in the mountains, the Coffeys kept hogs to butcher in the late fall months. Ruby said her daddy had a place where he salted the meat until it was cured before putting the meat inside a bag and hanging it up for future use. She said he also put a little borax on the meat to keep the insects from spoiling it. In addition to these cured hams and shoulders, the family supplemented their diet with the rabbits, squirrels, and pheasants her brothers hunted.

Ruby said that her mother, at fifteen years of age, had sewed all of her own clothes, and she continued to make clothes for her children when they were young. Eva had one of the old treadle machines that were powered by foot. The cotton sacks that feed came in were printed with colorful patterns, and women used them to make dresses and skirts.

Eva also loved to quilt and would visit other ladies in the holler, so that they could work on quilts together. Ruby's aunt, Nin
Coffey, told me that she had a quilting frame attached to ropes
that she lowered from the ceiling of their cabin when she wanted
to work on a new piece. When she was done, the frame was raised
back up, out of the way.

Ruby remembered that one of their neighbors, by the name of
Odie Demastus, smoked, and he bought his tobacco in little white
cloth bags. When the bags were empty, his wife, Effie, would dye
them different colors and use them to make patchwork quilt tops.
Ruby said that Effie made a pretty one that she had dyed yellow
and green.

Forest also worked
in the apple orchards
each year and hauled
workers back and
forth in his truck.
Ruby and many of her
friends and relatives
helped pick fruit to
earn extra money. She
remembers working
for her uncle Johnny
one year, picking
peaches in an orchard
across the mountain
near Afton.

I commented on
the dresses the girls
wore to work in,
and Ruby laughed
and said, "We didn't
know what a pair
of pants was back
then!" Ruby also
hired herself out as a

"Peach pickers": Ruby, Rachel Arnold, and Ora Coffey

common laborer, helping others hoe their corn. She remembers working for her neighbors Saylor Coffey and Gordon Demastus, who lived across the mountain in Page Hollow, for a dollar a day, and she thought she was making good money.

As a child, Ruby attended Ivy Hill School, which was located in the holler just up the road from her home. It was the same one-room schoolhouse that her father had attended when he was growing up; when the school was no longer in service, her brother Houston and his family lived in the building.

When it was first built, Ivy Hill had been made of logs, but by the time Ruby attended there, they had covered the logs with weatherboard. There was a woodstove located in the middle of the classroom that heated the building in the winter months. The teacher's desk was at the front on a raised platform, and there were enough windows providing light for the children to see their lessons. In the early years, the school had classes up to the seventh grade, but Ruby went only to the sixth grade at Ivy Hill and finished up the seventh at the school in Stuarts Draft.

She commented that they had some of the best "entertainments" (end-of-year school programs), in which the children participated in a play or some type of reading, and her dad, uncle Johnny, and aunt Mary and her husband Dewey Fitzgerald would make music.

Some of her teachers at that time were Pearl Allen, Edna Brydge, and Lillian Robertson. The teachers boarded with Ruby's family while school was in session, so they didn't have very far to travel each day.

At recess, the children played a game called "sticks," in which sticks were strategically placed around the building and whoever snuck around and gathered up the most was the winner. Another popular game was "Annie Over" ("Andover"), in which a ball was thrown back and forth over the roof to the children waiting on each side. At the time, Frank Stump had a sawmill down by the creek, and the kids loved to run down and play around it. In the winter, they loved to sleigh ride down a steep place in the road called "schoolhouse hill."

Christmas in the holler was always celebrated by having meals with all the relatives. On Christmas Eve, the Coffey children would put empty shoeboxes at the top of the stairs for Santa to fill. In the morning, there would be much excitement over the candy, oranges, pencils, and gloves found in their boxes. Unlike today, back then oranges were a seasonal fruit available only during the holidays.

Ruby said that she couldn't remember if the family decorated a live tree when she was small, but she recalls one Christmas Eve after she was of working age they got a tree, but the weather got so bad they couldn't get home that evening. They spent the night at her sister Louise's house and drove home on Christmas morning to set up the tree while Eva prepared a huge meal for the whole family to come and eat together that night.

People living in the holler when Ruby lived there were Ellis and Etta Everitt; Royal and Sadie Everitt; Zandy and Estie Coffey; Ruby's grandparents Tom and Nannie Coffey; Johnny and Nin Coffey; Odie, Effie, and Golden Demastus; Teressa, Joe, Saylor, Annie, and Billy Coffey; Henry and Millie Coffey; and Ruby's brother Houston and his family who by that time lived in the old Ivy Hill schoolhouse.

Another fond memory that came to Ruby while we were talking was of her parents' cabinet radio. "It was the first one in the holler, and on Saturday nights, after all the work was done and the supper dishes were washed, we would clean the chimneys on the oil lamps and put them back on the wall shelf before people started to come in. Zandy and Estie Coffey or Odie and Effie Demastus would come, and we would tune the radio in and listen to the Grand Ole Opry on the Nashville station. Mama would bring out a pan of apples to eat while we listened."

The family usually bought needed staples from the store in White Rock owned by Hercy Coffey. "There was a path just down from our home that came out at Pat and Quincey Coffey's place on the North Fork, and we'd walk up to Hercy's store from there." There was also a store at Love, in the rear of Henry Everitt's home, where they sometimes bought or traded goods.

Washing clothes was done by hand on an old-fashioned scrub board, the water having been heated on Eva's wood cookstove. The clean clothes were then strung on a line outside, and since the family didn't have the convenience of electricity, they were later ironed with flat irons that were also heated on the wood stove. Before they moved up to Love, the family hooked up to the electric line being strung through the holler. Eva acquired a wringer washing machine that made the chore of washing clothes a lot easier than scrubbing them on a washboard.

The Coffey family worshipped at Mountain Top Christian Church in Love, where Ruby has been a lifetime member. A new sanctuary was built in 1921 after the original log church, located across the Parkway on Campbell's Mountain Road, fell into disrepair. Ruby said that there was a cleared spot where the old church had stood where they used to hold family reunions. She showed me a colorful Sunday-school card that she had been given when she was nine years old by her teacher, Eva Hewitt, that was dated 1933.

Ruby said that Rev. John McKenney was the preacher who baptized her in the creek that ran through her family's property in the holler. Other preachers at the church were Davis Coffey, Bob Allen, Emmett Perry, and Mr. Harris. Although the family

An early funeral at Mountain Top Church

attended Mountain Top for Sunday services, they would also walk to the White Rock and Evergreen churches if they were having some type of special function.

Mountain Top has seen many changes over the years, includ-ing the additions of an entrance foyer, rear kitchen/Sunday school room, a picnic pavilion, and an indoor bathroom—although the two outdoor privies at the side of the church are still used when needed. Yearly homecoming services are still held at the church, as well as weddings and funerals.

Ruby's first job was at the blanket factory in Waynesboro. Because of the distance involved, and since Ruby had no vehicle of her own, she boarded during the workweek with her uncle and aunt who lived in Lyndhurst. Her brother Richard worked at the

Ruby at the old homeplace

same factory, and he would pick her up and bring her back in the evening. She would return home to the holler on the weekends.

Ruby with one of her cars

Ruby eventually bought a car of her own and remembers washing it in the creek where the water crossed a low spot in the road. Ellis Everitt lived in the house closest to the creek, and Ruby said that he'd walk down when she was washing the car and say, "That is a fine-looking machine you got there."

When the blanket factory was getting ready to close down, Ruby took a week's vacation and put in an application at the General Electric plant in Waynesboro. She was hired and went to work the following week, staying at the company for thirty-two years before retiring. Jesse Bridge had a large van that many of the GE employees, including Ruby, rode to work in. She retired in March 1987.

"Moving day 1961": Moving from the holler up to Love

Because the holler was so hard to get in and out of during the winter months, the decision was made to move up to the village of Love, a short distance away. Holler neighbors, Saylor and Annie Coffey, had made the move in 1953, and Forest's brother Johnny and his family had followed in 1955. Ruby's family moved in 1961, and they had a contract with the Jim Walter Company to build their new home. She said that Ralph and Jake Hewitt finished the basement and dug the water line from a spring across the road that brought water into a spring box and pumped it inside the house.

The Coffeys adapted to their new location and had many wonderful times over the years that they lived there. The extended family held annual picnics at Coyner Springs Park near Waynesboro that were always looked forward to and well attended.

In March 1984, I came up to take a photograph of Ruby, her parents, and Saylor and Johnny Coffey for a front cover of the April issue of the *Backroads* newspaper entitled, "The Folks from over in the Holler." I interviewed them all about what life was like growing up back in the mountains, and it continues to be one of my favorite stories in the twenty-five years that *Backroads* was published.

The Forest Coffey Family: (top) Houston, Eva, Forest, and Richard; (bottom) Louise, Madeline, and Ruby

Three years later, in March 1987, Ruby was honored at a GE retirement party for her thirty-two years of service. Without having to go to an outside job, Ruby settled down at home to help her parents, who were getting up in age, with daily activities.

Forest and Eva celebrated seventy-seven years of marriage before Eva passed away on

Coffey family picnic held at Coyner Springs Park

Ruby with her parents and Saylor and Johnny Coffey at their home in Love

January 17, 1994. Forest followed one year and five months later on June 7, 1995. Ruby stayed on at the homeplace throughout that winter, which turned out to be quite severe. So the decision was made in the spring of 1996 to move to a home in Sherando,

Ruby and her parents at her retirement party from GE

Ruby's parents, Forest and Eva Coffey (Love, Virginia)

next door to her great niece, Kim Mize, and her husband, David; she continues to reside there today. I remember that the ladies of Mountain Top Church gave Ruby a housewarming party when she moved, and we had such a good time watching her open all her gifts.

At this writing, Ruby, who will be eighty-nine years of age on August 13, is the oldest living person who grew up in the holler and spent most of her life in the community of Love, Virginia. Two of her best friends were Annie Coffey and Virgie Hewitt, who were neighbors who lived here on the mountain until their

Ruby at her 1996 housewarming party at Mountain Top Church

deaths. Annie was two years older than Ruby, so they grew up together and were very close throughout their lives. Virgie married Ralph Hewitt, whose family was from Love, and she spent the rest of her life here also. They called each other several times a day, attended church together, and Ruby misses them to this day.

But she is happy living next door to her niece's family, who take care of her needs and are so good to her.

Ruby said she has so many memories of living back in the hollow, and she summed up her feelings in one sentence: "I know we came up hard, but sometimes I miss it so much, I just have to cry thinking about how happy we were in the holler and all the people who lived there that are gone now."

Lillian Foster (Batesville)

Old stone chimney

The Chimney Still Stands
By "Preacher Billy" Morris

Does the ancient chimney still stand there?
Lifting itself proudly in the soft summer air;
I wonder each time as we journey so near,
Does it yet stand, or did it fall last year?

Then I behold it with happy eye
Above the landscape bold and high;
Near the green willows at the clearing's end
Across the small meadow by the river's bend.

Silent sentinel, there for all to see,
You're more than a lonely chimney to me;
A symbol of enduring strength thou art,
A strong tower of hope within my heart.

There is much in life that falls to decay,
Disappoints and fails us and passes away;
Faith, hope, and love like that chimney sure
When all else is gone, will still endure.

Oft the plans we cherish like old houses fall,
The porch, the roof, and, at last, the wall;
Like that old chimney with foundation of stone,
The life built on Christ will forever live on.

About the Author

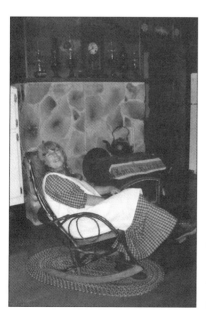

Even as a child, Lynn Coffey had a Waldenish bent toward a nineteenth-century existence, despite the fact that she was growing up along the busy Gold Coast of southern Florida, with all the amenities of modern living. Her dream was to build a log cabin in the mountains and live a quiet, self-sufficient lifestyle.

Lynn began living that dream upon moving to the tiny hamlet of Love, Virginia, in the summer of 1980. As she met and got to know her neighbors, all of whom were quite elderly at the time, she soon realized the culture of these hearty Scottish/Irish descendants was slowly ebbing away and somehow needed to be preserved.

Without any formal education or prior experience in journalism, Lynn carved out a folksy niche, documenting early Appalachian life through the pages of a monthly newspaper she created called *Backroads*, the first issue being published in December 1981.

For the next twenty-five years, *Backroads* chronicled the history of the mountain people as Lynn traveled the hills and hollers, interviewing the native elders and photographing handicrafts and activities that had been handed down for generations.

In the process, little did she realize how entwined her life would become with theirs or how much the mountain people would come to mean to her as they opened their hearts and trusted a young woman who started out as an "outsider" and ended up becoming one of them.

When Lynn retired from the newspaper in December of 2006, the mountain people's cry, "Don't let our stories die with your retirement," haunted her, and she began compiling the articles from the old newspaper, putting them in book form. Three books about the Appalachian culture resulted: *Plain Folk and Simple Livin'*, *The Road to Chicken Holler*, and *Faces of Appalachia*. The newest, *Appalachian Heart*, is written for the last generation of people from the Virginia highlands who grew up the old way.

You can order additonal copies of *Appalachian Heart* or other books by Lynn Coffey by using this order form.

ORDER FORM

Name _____

Address _____

City, State, Zip _____

Appalachian Heart	_____	copies
Backroads	_____	copies
Backroads 2	_____	copies
Backroads 3	_____	copies

The price of each book is $20.00. Please add $5.00 for shipping for each copy ordered. Make checks or money orders payable to Lynn Coffey and mail to:

Lynn Coffey
1461 Love Road
Lyndhurst, VA 22952
www.backroadsbooks.com